He is the One

Lost and Found

Ramzy Fakhouri

WESTBOW
PRESS®
A DIVISION OF THOMAS NELSON
& ZONDERVAN

Scripture quotations are from the ESV® Bible (The Holy Bible, English Standard Version®), copyright © 2001 by Crossway, a publishing ministry of Good News Publishers. Used by permission. All rights reserved.

This book is a work of non-fiction. Unless otherwise noted, the author and the publisher make no explicit guarantees as to the accuracy of the information contained in this book and in some cases, names of people and places have been altered to protect their privacy.

WestBow Press books may be ordered through booksellers or by contacting:

WestBow Press
A Division of Thomas Nelson & Zondervan
1663 Liberty Drive
Bloomington, IN 47403
www.westbowpress.com
844-714-3454

Because of the dynamic nature of the Internet, any web addresses or links contained in this book may have changed since publication and may no longer be valid. The views expressed in this work are solely those of the author and do not necessarily reflect the views of the publisher, and the publisher hereby disclaims any responsibility for them.

Any people depicted in stock imagery provided by Thinkstock are models, and such images are being used for illustrative purposes only. Certain stock imagery © Thinkstock.

ISBN: 978-1-5127-6078-1 (sc)
ISBN: 978-1-5127-6079-8 (hc)
ISBN: 978-1-5127-6080-4 (e)

Library of Congress Control Number: 2016917275

Print information available on the last page.

WestBow Press rev. date: 09/17/2021

Contents

Introduction

If you are looking for a religious book of rules and rituals then this is certainly not the book for you. If you are looking for a book that you can read to just pass the time this is not for you either. This book will challenge: make you glad, sad, and maybe even mad. You will not leave indifferent after reading. It is for both the unbeliever, and the believer in God. It is for atheists, agnostics, and theists of all kinds. It is for the Muslim, Buddhist, Jew, Christian, and all the many different worshipers in the world. It is for the people who don't know God, think they know him, and those who truly know him. This book is for the ones who call themselves spiritual, not religious, and for those who are searching. It is for Democrat, Republican, and Independent: for Pro-life and Pro-Choice. It is for the destitute and the silver-spooned. Whether you are looked down on as in the fringes of society, looked upon as an elitist, or anywhere else in between; It is surely a book for the Lost and Found.

"Amazing grace! How sweet the sound
That saved a wretch like me!
I once was lost, but now am found,
Was blind but now I see."

This excerpt of the hymn, <u>Amazing Grace</u>, published in 1779, by a man named John Newton, is still very popular and many of us may have heard it sung, and may not have even realized it. What is significant about it is what it portrays. It speaks to someone who was previously lost in life, and having been found; and that by God.

We live in this world and are looking and searching for meaning and purpose, and many of us are still looking for their fulfillment. Many are looking and yet feeling lost in the shuffle as we contemplate the meaning of life. It is drudgery at best for most of us, with many fleeting moments of passing victories, and then with emptiness setting back in. And then the search continues, but through all the toil the seeker still feels lost.

Many of us are looking to find our place in the world, yet we suppress our true condition. We may pridefully proclaim, "I'm not lost. I'm just looking to find myself." When all the time, deep down in our souls, our consciences proclaim, "I am so lost." That was me. I was certainly lost, but did not want to admit it.

The hymn speaks to me in so many ways. It speaks to my own time of being lost without God, and to the time where I was found. It speaks to my own toils in all my conquests while trying to find fulfillment in the pleasures that my hands, or eyes could lay themselves on so as to not feel the emptiness of being lost in life. It certainly speaks to my trying to keep my mind occupied with all kinds of distractions so as to not sit quiet with my conscience that was not at peace within me. The lostness of the emptiness of life kept me wanting more, and the insatiable desires within me became like a vacuum.

Through a multitude of pitfalls in life, I was brought to the lowest point that I could ever go. But there was something different this time, at my lowest, than all the other times of feeling lost, misunderstood, trapped, and broken. It was a hungering for, and a searching after God.

I did not know God, but was seeking. My seeking was there, but initially the content of my search was not. Reading the Holy Bible was surely a strange place for me, but during that time I was also exposed to opposing doctrines from false teachers that were contrary to the biblical teaching, but were surely religious. I started having a spiritual life and experiences, but not from God; though the whole time thinking I knew him, and trying to please him. I had no direction, and my life started to spiral out of control.

This may not be your story at all, and that is okay. This is a glimpse into my story prior to being found by God, who delivered me from falsehood of all kinds and transformed my life, giving me hope, peace, and purpose; one of which is to write this book to reach many with the universal message that transforms people around the globe, and throughout the centuries. Within this book is a culmination of a series of devotionals that God put on my heart to share on social media, and now with all of you in this way. The message in this book is to speak to many with the good news that gave me the greatest hope and changed my life, and can change yours too. It is geared to people who may feel lost or searching. It is intended for all who are seeking to find the true meaning and hope in life. It is in the one true God; he is to be found, by all who are seeking wholeheartedly, being drawn by him.

I have found that Jesus Christ is the One I did not know that I had needed to find, but through seeking God with all my heart, found that he was the One seeking me. In fact, through the following core message of the many that is shared with you, God found me. No word play, no stretch. God revealed to me, through his revelation of good news from heaven, that I needed him, and was extending this great and immeasurable love, clarity, and fulfillment for my life in him through this good news, by his grace.

"I once was lost, but now am found,
Was blind but now I see."

Picture finding out that your Creator loves you and grants eternal life; lavishing this great favor on lost, broken, hopeless, and undeserving souls. Imagine finding out that the purpose for life can be known to you, and that you can have peace and joy, and be found, through good news, and be made complete; the vacuum of the soul filled where you once were empty.

This book is also meant to encourage, and all the more equip the found, that they may be all the more emboldened to share the preciousness of the message with many others, who maybe have not shared their faith in a while, or maybe have yet to, being another way to convey God's love for the lost and found.

No matter where you are at, I invite you to read. Each chapter points to the One and only, who loves and who lives. Whether you have never opened a Bible, found the Scriptures completely not understandable, or find Christianity strange or foreign to you: hold on. This book is geared to share the faith with clarity, and in all love, in each chapter.

With each short chapter read, you can put the book down and not miss a beat when reading the others. Each has a purpose, and each may speak to certain people differently than others, but the theme throughout is steadfast.

Again, I can assure you it is not a religious book for ritual seekers who are looking to check off some spiritual box, and most certainly is not fiction, but is truthful, and may even be used by God to bring transformation and hope to your life. The message inside brought me from faithlessness, bondage, and vain religiosity, to faith, deliverance, and relationship with God.

My prayer, my dear friends, is that you may be found by the One who is seeking for the lost. May you be found by the One who is the God of love, and is so good. May he draw you close and reveal himself to you that you too can cast aside the preconceived, and be found in the God given faith. Whether happy or sad, glad or mad, lost or found, my hope is that you may all have good news always, and forever, for he is the One.

Your friend in Christ,
Ramzy

1

···

What is Truth?

What is truth? Do you know? Some may laugh at the question, but after taking some time to think about it, they cannot really come up with an answer. We live in a generation where relativism and similar philosophies dominate. The philosophy of relativism teaches that what is right for you and what is right for me can be completely different, and there is no absolute truth. We claim we know so much that surely we know truth. But do we?

When people are to take the stand in a courtroom, they take an oath to tell the truth. When we speak contrary to truth, our consciences convict us. We have not told the truth. There is the utmost importance to us all in answering this question: What is truth?

Some people believe that whatever they say is the truth. In the movie, Scarface, the actor Al Pacino stated, "I always tell the truth. Even when I lie." Other people are exposed to the truth yet continue on with what they've got. Winston Churchill, a British prime minister, speaking of another, was quoted by Reader's Digest Magazine saying, "Occasionally he stumbled over the truth but he always picked himself up and hurried on as if nothing had happened." So what's so important about truth, you might ask. I believe the author C. S. Lewis said it best in his book, A Grief

<u>Observed</u>, when he wrote, "You never know how much you really believe anything until its truth or falsehood becomes a matter of life and death to you."

'..."*What is truth?*"...' *(John 18:38)* Pontius Pilate, a Roman governor, asked what would have been a wise question of Jesus Christ. Unfortunately Pilate didn't know truth when the Truth was looking at and speaking to him. Before he asked this question, Jesus had said, '...*"For this purpose I have come into the world—to bear witness to the truth. Everyone who is of the truth listens to my voice."'* *(John 18:37)* May we be responders rather than rejecters of the truth.

Jesus was '...*'full of grace and truth"* *(John 1:14)* and proclaimed, '..."*I am the way, and the truth...*" *(John 14:6)* Notice he didn't say *a* truth, but *the* truth. In the book of Revelation, Jesus is called Faithful and True and that his words are trustworthy and true. He has certainly come to set the captives free. Who are these captives, you might ask. Those who have been lost and living in error, falsehood, and their own "truth," which is sin.

For almost thirty-five, years I lived as I pleased and thought of myself as pretty righteous. Sure, I lied a lot and did things I knew were wrong, but not many people knew about what I did or what I thought. In my eyes, I was pretty nice to people and called myself a Christian. Hey, I was born into a Christian-professing family and wore a cross around my neck. Yet I was an angry and rageful person, never mind a drunk, to say the least. My life could be summed up with a line from the <u>My Way</u> song sung by Frank Sinatra: "I did it my way." Like many people, I thought that didn't matter much. Not until I came face-to-face with, and could no longer escape, the truth.

The truth was that we have sinned against a righteous and holy God and '...*'the wages of sin is death...'* *(Romans 6:23)*. That means that sinning once has made us guilty before God, and we are on a collision course with eternity. That eternity is in a place of '...

weeping and gnashing of teeth' (Matthew 13:42) called hell. Some churches try to teach the contrary about hell with a place called purgatory, but it is not found in God's word. Some believe that by good deeds or by doing right in their own sight, or in the sight of others, they could earn salvation or impress God.

Jesus came to die on the cross, and his sacrifice is sufficient for the lost to be found. Jesus came to save sinners like us from the power of sin in our lives by taking the punishment for his creation on himself. He came to save sinful people like me from my sins. There weren't enough good deeds I could have done or enough charities I could have given to. My problem was with the question "What is truth?" My truth was what I thought was right, what felt good at the moment, without much fear of consequences for my actions. I figured as long as I stayed out of jail, what harm was done with my "truth"? I feared man more than God.

The good news is that the wrath due sinners was poured out on Christ on the cross, and that is the reason why he came. Only the One called the Truth could pay the penalty for sinners to be set free. Only One who is perfect and blameless would do. Though sinless and truthful in every way, Jesus took the full punishment for our sinfulness. This is what is meant by the passage, *'For our sake he made him to be sin who knew no sin, so that in him we might become the righteousness of God.' (2 Corinthians 5:21)* God did this because of his love. He took the full penalty at the cross two thousand years ago and grants eternal life to all of us who turn, and believe, providing the righteousness of Jesus Christ to all who live by faith.

Testimony is declaration of truth. In God's word in the Holy Bible it states, *'...this is the testimony, that God gave us eternal life, and this life is in his Son. Whoever has the Son has life; whoever does not have the Son of God does not have life.' (1 John 5:11-12)* Do you know the truth?

What I said I believed and what was actually in my heart were two different things. I said I believed in God but had no real reverent fear of him because of love, respect, and awe by grace, so I did not listen to him. I felt as though I were the center of the universe. I said I believed in him but didn't know truth. I was living in error, and my life was a testimony completely opposite of it. When I was faced with the truth of God's holy word in the gospel, he transformed my life. I became aware of my sinfulness and that Jesus's righteousness and salvation by his death on the cross and resurrection from death was extended to and drawing me. I came to know the truth, and the truth liberated me. I was lost, and God found me. I came to have repentance and relationship rather than rituals and religion, and that with Jesus. God had sent me the Holy Spirit, the Spirit of truth! I had a healthy reverent fear of God, who has the power over life and death and wanted me to live. He loved this sinner so much that he died in my place and wants those that he died for to be forgiven and live forever with him. God is the One *'who desires all people to be saved and to come to the knowledge of the truth.' (1 Timothy 2:4)* So the question to you stands. What is truth? Will you believe the Truth or hold on to your "truth"? Will you receive or reject it? This separates those lost to those found. What is truth?

Some say, like I did, that they believe, yet live contrary to God's standard. Jesus said, *"'...repent and believe...'" (Mark 1:15)*. Some are *'always learning and never able to arrive at the knowledge of the truth.' (2 Timothy 3:7)* There are people who are aware of their sinfulness but have yet to receive Christ as their Lord and Savior. Others are hell bent on doing things their own way. The command stands, *"'... repent and believe...'" (Mark 1:15).* In 1 John 1:6-8, God's word says,

'If we say we have fellowship with him while we walk in darkness, we lie and do not practice the truth. But if we walk in the light, as he is in the light, we have fellowship with one another, and the blood of Jesus

his Son cleanses us from all sin. If we say we have no sin, we deceive ourselves, and the truth is not in us.'

It's easy to say I love you. That's why it also says, *'...let us not love in word or talk but in deed and in truth.' (1 John 3:18)* The truth about who we are and the truth about who he is and what he has done for sinners has transforming power, by faith, to set us free from the bondage of sin and death.

Truth can be uncomfortable to those who thought they had the "truth." Truth can cause some to stiffen their neck because they refuse to believe the truth. Some get angry when confronted with the truth. Others bend to the crowd and turn from the truth. Pontius Pilate handed over the Truth to be crucified. The unrighteous suppress the truth. Unfortunately many *'...exchanged the truth about God for a lie...' (Romans 1:25).* Truth flies in the face of preconceived notions. Truth brings a change to those who receive it. Truth brings a straight path to those who live by it. Truth brings a transformation to those who have truly known it. God's word says, *'...you will know the truth, and the truth will set you free."' (John 8:32)* What is *your* truth?

Elvis Presley once said "Truth is like the sun. You can shut it out for a time, but it ain't goin' away." What is truth? Friend, I pray that this would be a new year with truth directing your every step. My prayer is that you would know the meaning of life and live with purpose every day. I pray you would read the word of truth, the Holy Bible, and find all the blessings of heaven and love in Christ from this day forward and into eternity. May we all be found in him who is in the kingdom of heaven, and escape the wide open mouth of hell. Receive him, reject him, but be sure you cannot run from the Truth.

2

....

The Good Advocate

'My little children, I am writing these things to you so that you
may not sin. But if anyone does sin, we have an advocate with the
Father, Jesus Christ the righteous. He is the propitiation for our
sins, and not for ours only but also for the sins of the whole world.
And by this we know that we have come to know him, if we keep
his commandments. Whoever says "I know him" but does not
keep his commandments is a liar, and the truth is not in him, but
whoever keeps his word, in him truly the love of God is perfected.
By this we may know that we are in him: whoever says he abides
in him ought to walk in the same way in which he walked.'
(1 John 2:1-6)
-the word of God

'Can the Ethiopian change his skin or the leopard his spots? Then also
you can do good who are accustomed to do evil.' (Jeremiah 13:23)
God's word gives this analogy, and we can visualize the futility
in thinking a person can, with a thought, change his skin color
from black to white or an animal changing from spots to stripes,
and comparing that to a person changing their heart or mind to
do real good when someone practices evil. Can a person change

themselves? Can someone who is accustomed to sin change? Can someone who quit smoking also quit sinning? I remember feeling particularly sinful at a time in my life, and so I finally went with my mom to a local church. I may have made it 2 or 3 times. And guess what happened? Nothing: I was looking to clean myself up and try to do some self-help with religion so nothing happened. My heart remained unchanged. We sin and that is what we know. We may try to act religious or do good deeds when we feel guilty for our sin but it does not change the fact that the sin is still there. What do we think about sin?

Well, here in God's word we hear what God says about sin. What is sin? We may know that we sin but not know what it means, which is missing the mark. It can also be defined as, to miss or wander from the path of uprightness and honor, or to do or go wrong. This sin that we may be indifferent to and may even find thrilling is what God considers lawlessness. Whether it be looking with lust which God considers adultery, earnestly desiring what our neighbors have that we do not, which is called coveting, bearing false witness about our neighbor, stealing, or any other of the commandments we break when God said we should not it is called sin. It is found in us whenever we do the opposite of what God said to do or not to do. This sin causes the greatest chasm between us and God and due to our sin we have no relationship. The word of God says '...*your iniquities have made a separation between you and your God, and your sins have hidden his face from you so that he does not hear.*' *(Isaiah 59:2)* Have you ever cried out to God for help and nothing happened and received no answer? Have you called out to God but it was as if you were praying to the wind? Did your prayers reach the ceiling and go no further? It is due to the thing common in all of humanity. Indeed, '...*all have sinned and fall short of the glory of God...*' *(Romans 3:23).*

So our sins separate us from God and cuts off all access to our cries for help: Is that it? I cannot know my Creator because of my sin? No, not only that, but '...*the wages of sin is death...*' (Romans 6:23). Our God is holy, and righteous, and perfect. Our missing the mark of God's standard of perfection pronounces us guilty of rebellion against God. No matter your religion or your disbelief of God, you will answer to him. When we die, we will give an account for our lives. If we would have no one to intercede for us that death will be in the depths of eternal hell, a place of fire, torment, and darkness. Hell is a place where all lawbreakers go. You need an advocate, someone to intercede on your side. Do you know Jesus?

"Wait a minute," you might say. "I only have 'little sins' or 'little white lies.' I'm not as bad as others. I'm pretty moral and do a lot of good works. I try to keep the commandments...sometimes." My friend, you are making the biggest leap to try to reach God by your own ability and strength, but reality pulls you back. God's word tells us, '*We have all become like one who is unclean, and all our righteous deeds are like a polluted garment. We all fade like a leaf, and our iniquities, like the wind, take us away.*' (Isaiah 64:6) I tried when I went those two or three times to clean myself up at church, but couldn't, and neither can you. We can by no means earn our salvation. We will be judged by the law, the ten commandments, and the law demands perfection.

What can a person do to save themselves? This is how great our God is; he has sent good news for sinners from heaven. God is not only the Holy Judge but also merciful and loving, and he has provided one way for the world to be set free from sin and have a saving relationship with him. He has provided the only way for the stain of sin to be lifted off you and me and to wipe the slate clean. There is one way to have intercession with God the Father and that is only through his Son Jesus. Jesus said these wonderful words.

"For God so loved the world, that he gave his only Son, that whoever believes in him should not perish but have eternal life."' (John 3:16) God has provided the propitiation: the offering satisfying the laws demands for sin, and that is by becoming a man in the perfect person of Jesus Christ and dying in place. The God that we offended who is perfectly righteous must punish sin, for he is a Righteous Judge and sin is lawlessness. God, who will carry out justice for the sin against him and must punish the doers of sin is the same God that delights to forgive and justify the ungodly through faith in his Son, by his grace that is given to those who do not deserve it. The One without sin came to make satisfaction for the sins of wicked people, absorbing the penalty and wrath for his people on the cross through his death. Someone perfect was needed to break the curse of sin for lawbreakers that we may have access to the Father, by faith, and an advocate when we miss the mark. He is the One named Jesus who rose from the dead. The One very willing to be our Advocate when believers fall short is the One who became the living sacrifice for sin. He sets sinners free from condemnation and judgment if we believe in the Lord Jesus. We need life and that life is in his Son.

Jesus commands, *"…repent and believe in the gospel." (Mark 1:15)* Repent is to change one's mind. It's to change your course and head in a totally different direction. To believe in the gospel is to believe in the good news that the One who loves sinners, your God and Creator, is the very One who came into this world to make full payment for your sins in the person of Jesus Christ, that we wouldn't have to pay. With child-like faith we can, by God's undeserved gift, be transformed and given a new life through faith in Jesus, and be filled with the Holy Spirit. We will be completely forgiven and no longer condemned for judgment and eternal hell. We will have access and an Advocate with the Father through Jesus Christ the Righteous. You will have the assurance of God that when you die you too will go home to heaven to be with him, and live forever at peace with God because the life of Jesus is counted to you. When we believe we receive it all. He will be with us while living throughout our lives now on earth, and to declare us not guilty by his blood when we fall short. He brought me to repentance and faith and provided this new life for me while not deserving it and provided me with new heart desires: those that please my God.

What if some claim to know God yet there is no change in their lives? God is by no means fooled. Jesus said, *"This people honors me with their lips, but their heart is far from me..."* *(Matthew 15:8)*. God's word calls them a liar. Many also pray to so many others and may say many prayers but do not know Jesus. They follow man made religions and traditions, and not the true faith found in the word of God.

This is the proof of the transformed life and God given faith, that we follow his word and keep his commandments. Being justified by faith alone we can now live by God's grace and '...*uphold the law...*' *(Romans 3:31)* that we once lived to break continually, and this as Jesus continues as our faithful and good Advocate. The gift of faith gives us knowledge that this faith is completely and freely given by God and liberates us from trying to earn our salvation and from the sin that will destroy us. And it is completely a supernatural event that God does as he works righteousness in all who believe. Our lives are no longer sin continually and living a lifestyle of sin, but have God working within us. Our lives become more like Jesus, causing us to now live by the power of his word through his Spirit in ways pleasing to him. And when we miss the mark we have Jesus interceding for us, for we have access to confession and repentance, and the promise that God will hear and welcome us. When God looks at us he sees Jesus' perfect track record. We have God with us, with Jesus Christ in our corner, with his promise to never leave or forsake us. We have access and peace with God, and are given understanding of his holy word.

My dear friend, believe in God and be set free from your sin and rejoice with me in the new life in Jesus Christ, being found in him. The Bible says, '...*he died for all, that those who live might no longer live for themselves but for him who for their sake died and was raised.*' *(2 Corinthians 5:15)*

3

....

How Valuable You Are To God

'Because you are precious in my eyes, and honored, and I love you…'
(Isaiah 43:4)
-the word of God

Everyone who was brought into saving faith in God has a conversion story where life has been radically transformed, and in a moment becoming new. I had the privilege of meeting two missionaries from church in America to Japan, on a return trip, and a Japanese Christian musician who came to visit with them from there as well. After hearing and being grateful for what God was doing in Japan through our Christian family there, this artist shared her testimony of coming to faith in Jesus. She went to church in Japan as she did so many times before. But something was different that day. She heard this passage. *'Because you are precious in my eyes, and honored, and I love you…' (Isaiah 43:4).* Deeply depressed and living with the feeling of worthlessness for some time, she was touched by God as only he could touch someone. She came to know that she had value with God. She came to know that God loved her, in spite of her low self-worth: that she was precious to him and she was honored. That was the Scripture that God used to open her heart and reveal his great love for her.

The God of creation is the God who loves sinners in spite of our sins against him. He is a God of salvation who sends good news of his Son, and would rather us repent and turn to him, than judge our wickedness. He is a gift giver and the God to lift us up by grace, calling all to believe, rather than to give us justice and cast us down. He grants forgiveness and heaven than judgment and hell for those who believe. He gives us peace and joy *now* through a relationship with him by faith, than us continuing to carry depression and distress without him. He is the God who made you in his very image and loves sinners, not wanting to see any he loves to perish in their sin. He is the God who wants relationship, as a loving Father with his child, for he has made his creation for him. He sent his Son that the ungodly may be forgiven. The receivers of his grace are that precious to God, that we may know we are his, and know where we are going.

God came down from heaven, through Jesus, conceived by the Holy Spirit through the miracle virgin birth, to take the punishment deserved, that believers may have fellowship with him. He reaches down with the gospel call, the good news, and sends his people with his message to reach all, that many may be lifted up by faith. He justifies those who believe in his Son through his life, death, and resurrection from the dead. He sent his Son in place of all who would believe, to bear punishment for sinners on the cross through his death. He clothes believers with the righteousness of Christ. This righteousness is counted by the gift of faith from God.

He is calling the undeserving into relationship with him, to have a change of mind about sin, and to have faith that Jesus was delivered up for us. God does not want those Christ died for to receive justice for sin, but rather forgiveness because Jesus paid the penalty. He would rather you have peace with him than pain without. He sent his Son down to die on a cross in place. Why? This passage of God's love for his people reveals the heart of God for all who would believe. *'Because you are precious in my eyes, and honored, and I love you...' (Isaiah 43:4).* He reaches down with the gift of favor that is unmerited. Do not resist this awesome message of salvation through Jesus. Tomorrow is not promised. *'...Behold, now is the favorable time; behold, now is the day of salvation.' (2 Corinthians 6:2)*

4

....

What Do We Think About Abortion?

The topic came up during a semester at nursing school with classmates and the teacher. What do we think about abortion? It surely had been on my mind quite a bit. My mind has changed on it considerably before coming to faith in Jesus Christ. I was a young man with a girlfriend who was living for the moment. I thought about what was pleasing to me. I wanted the benefits of a relationship with a girlfriend without the commitment or responsibility. In my selfishness, when learning of the pregnancy, let her know I was not ready for a baby, maybe by telling her how this would be unacceptable to my family without being married, and so we agreed on an abortion. I took her to the place, we walked by a "wacko" with his religion who was there, outside the building, to try to prevent us from going into that place where abortions were performed, and a little while later, after walking her inside, it was over.

My girlfriend was traumatized, and could barely stand looking at me. She and I were riddled with guilt after. "What a coward," I thought to myself. "That could have been my son or my daughter." The thought, at first, was the false promise of freedom from the fear of change in my lifestyle but truly ended with great regret. It gave the facade of something sweet but the guilt became like bitterness in my stomach. My conscience became my enemy. I knew I was wrong.

I found myself thinking about it over and over whenever I saw my friends or other young couples with their children. "What if" would come to mind, and "I wish I never did" too. The remorse was there, but the guilt would not go away.

Over ten years had gone by. The unmendable relationship with the girlfriend became a memory. I moved on with life without her yet the pain would not go. My conscience continued to remind me. And then something happened. I did something out of the norm for me. Due to someone who tried to influence me to do so, I started reading the bible, and from the beginning.

When I finally got to the ten commandments of God it was there that I read these words: "*You shall not murder.*" *(Exodus 20:13)* It was like the words jumped off the page at me. At that moment it was like God had looked directly into my most hidden thoughts. My secret I called abortion was revealed through God's word for what it really was: murder. There I was, exposed, naked before Almighty God who sees all things. I had this immediate and undeniable sense that God was there, in the very room, and that he had found me out. He knew my secret. He knew of my murder. He knew I took what was not mine to take; the life of my baby boy or girl: my child.

In the book of Genesis, the first book in the Bible, it says, '… *God created man in his own image, in the image of God he created him; male and female he created them.' (Genesis 1:27)* The Creator of heaven and earth, the sun, the moon, and the stars, created that baby in the womb, having done so wonderfully, and I took the child's life.

'As you do not know the way the spirit comes to the bones in the womb of a woman with child, so you do not know the work of God who makes everything.' (Ecclesiastes 11:5)

Yes, without a doubt, no matter how we try to justify it, God considers his creation in the womb to be a child, a life given by him, and not to be destroyed by a parent, or anyone else, but rather protected. The tears streamed down my face as the remorse and guilt over the exposing of my sin by Holy God was unbearable. I buckled as I could no longer stand up. I knelt down, and prayed before God.

Jesus said these words, *"'...'You shall not murder; and whoever murders will be liable to judgment.'"* (Matthew 5:21) Here I was, a person who called myself a Christian, yet I had lived like the devil. That was only one of the ten commandments, and enough to send me to hell for all of eternity. My guilt was undeniable. I was exposed.

Some may say things to justify themselves for supporting abortion, but in reality it is more like swallowing a knife. It cuts deep, and we will eventually give an account to God who is holy, and judges righteously. Jesus said, *"Nothing is covered up that will not be revealed, or hidden that will not be known. Therefore whatever you have said in the dark shall be heard in the light, and what you have whispered in private rooms shall be proclaimed on the housetops."* (Luke 12:2-3) Do we hear the words of God speaking to us? Are we voicing our support to this very thing? He is the same one who said *"I tell you, on the day of judgment people will give account for every careless word they speak, for by your words you will be justified, and by your words you will be condemned."* (Matthew 12:36-37)

This same righteous and just God who avenges the ones that are defenseless also is loving kind and known for his mercy and grace. It is not something we deserve or can earn. The One who taught us about sin, condemnation, and hell, also taught us about righteousness, salvation, and heaven. Jesus said, *"Come to me, all who labor and are heavy laden, and I will give you rest. Take my yoke upon you, and learn from me, for I am gentle and lowly in heart, and you will find rest for your souls. For my yoke is easy, and my burden is light."* (Matthew 11:28-30)

"...Repent and believe..." (Mark 1:15). He came with the command for us to change our mind. He came to save men, women, and children. He came to save us from a life of sin and shame. The Lord Jesus came down from heaven to earth to pay the penalty we could not, taking away our guilt, and counting his righteousness to all who would believe on him, receiving his free gift of salvation. He said, *"'For God so loved the world, that he gave his only Son, that whoever believes in him should not perish but have eternal life. For God did not send his Son into the world to condemn the world, but in order that the world might be saved through him. Whoever believes in him is not condemned, but whoever does not believe is condemned already, because he has not believed in the name of the only Son of God.'" (John 3:16-18)*

I came weary and heavy burdened. I came guilty of murder, and ashamed. Although deserving judgment and eternal punishment, this holy, loving, and gracious God forgave me all of my sin and has taken away all the guilt. My soul has found rest, and that in Jesus Christ. He wants to forgive the repentant and believing from what we have done and what we have supported. He wants us to have a change of mind and take away our shame, and that our children may be safe inside, and also live outside of the womb.

He has already made payment for sinners to be set free by his sinless body two thousand years ago as he hung on the cross. Grace is there for all who receive the good news. A new life awaits those who would forsake their way and follow after the One who rose from the grave, the only One who can forgive sin. We would not have to pay the penalty for our sins with an eternity in hell, but have life for eternity. We would receive beauty for ashes. That is the message before us and that from God who loves. I pray we would receive a changing of mind about the murder of a child and receive the gift of a new life from the One who rose from the dead, so we too can rise. *"'If anyone has ears to hear, let them hear.'" (Mark 4:23)*

5

Look and Live

"'You have heard that it was said, 'You shall not commit adultery.' But I say to you that everyone who looks at a woman with lustful intent has already committed adultery with her in his heart. If your right eye causes you to sin, tear it out and throw it away. For it is better that you lose one of your members than that your whole body be thrown into hell.'"
(Matthew 5:27-29)
-Jesus Christ the Righteous

Wow! Many of us would look at adultery as infidelity; a relationship of affair with someone other than their marriage partner, between a husband and wife. When Jesus shares with us about the commandment, *'...'you shall not commit adultery,'' (Exodus 20:14)* he tells us an example of what adultery means on a deeper level. He said, *"'...everyone who looks at a woman with lustful intent has already committed adultery with her in his heart.'" (Matthew 5:28)* What God is revealing to us is that many of us who believe that we have not committed adultery have done so, and may even do it continually. Jesus is not only talking about a man looking at a woman with lust, but this example includes any lustful act of adultery such as a woman looking at a man lustfully, and also if you have looked with lust towards the same sex. You have fallen into the same condemnation as if having a relationship outside of the sanctity of marriage between a male and a female, a husband and wife, with that person you have looked lustfully upon, and have become a lawbreaker in the sight of God.

God also shows us the destructiveness, severity of, and God's seriousness about sin. *"If your right eye causes you to sin, tear it out and throw it away. For it is better that you lose one of your members than that your whole body be thrown into hell."* *(Matthew 5:29)*

This goes against our very human nature, and that's why God reveals our condition to us. Is Jesus talking about dismemberment here? Surely not. Is God revealing this to us so as to destroy us? No. "Who will pay for my sin? How will I be forgiven?" He reveals it so that we would recognize our sinfulness, our desperate need of a Savior, and to turn from our lawless way. One of the proverbs says it best, *'Sheol and Abaddon are never satisfied, and never satisfied are the eyes of man.'* *(Proverbs 27:20)* Notice the connection between the insatiable appetite of the names synonymous with death and destruction, Sheol and Abaddon, and how it is compared to the unappeasable appetite of what we take in by our sight.

We live in a society where every titillating visual picture is thrown in our view, whether we were looking for it or not. We are living in a time that at a click of a button all the nakedness and hedonistic actions and sins of others are seen. We may not see that their sins become ours when we do not turn away, and in God's sight we are storing up wrath for the Day of Judgment. There will be no one on that Day who will be able to say, "so and so tempted me." Each will bear the guilt individually, and the punishment has been decreed, an eternity in hell.

The word of God calls these, the lusts of the eyes and flesh, and that these desires are not from God, but are worldly and unspiritual. Due to our sinfulness we seem to think, *"Stolen water is sweet, and bread eaten in secret is pleasant."* *(Proverbs 9:17)* "If I just sneak a peek, if I just look when no one else is looking, if I just let my mind wander, what sin is that? No one gets hurt." But God says, *"I the Lord search the heart and test the mind, to give every man according to his ways, according to the fruit of his deeds."* *(Jeremiah 17:10)* We wrongly rationalize that the intent of our hearts and minds are unknown to God, or that he does not see what we do in secret. We will give an account.

Well, what about this world today? Can't we pass the blame on our environment? No. And why not? Jesus tells us why it's us. *"For from within, out of the heart of man, come evil thoughts, sexual immorality, theft, murder, adultery, coveting, wickedness, deceit, sensuality, envy, slander, pride, foolishness. All these evil things come from within, and they defile a person."* *(Mark 7:21-23)* So we can't blame society, we can't blame the world, nor blame our spouse, or the internet. We have all been given a choice, and all have chosen wrongly. *'The heart is deceitful above all things, and desperately sick; who can understand it?'* *(Jeremiah 17:9)* God came down to pay the penalty for sin on the cross and defeat death by rising from the dead to heal us from our sick and diseased hearts, so as to give us new hearts that beat for him, filling us with the Holy Spirit through faith in the Lord Jesus. Do you know him?

This sin of adultery is appointing many to the condemnation of hell. Surely we are being inundated with more corruption on television, on the internet, and while simply walking down the street. We either are looking lustfully at others, or are looking to be the object of desire in our lack of clothing and choice of dress. No, I am not talking about legalism, in trying to conform everyone to a certain kind of dress or bondage to my personal standard, but reality in the sight of God. We have forgotten how to blush.

What can we do? God reveals we should be looking to the cross, where we can find forgiveness, and be cleansed from our sins against God and against our very bodies. God took upon himself sin in the person of Jesus, and the wrath due for sin. He shed his righteous blood on the cross. Jesus Christ said, *"'Greater love has no one than this, that someone lay down his life for his friends.'" (John 15:13)* Our God is loving kind, showing steadfast love and mercy, giving undeserving men and women grace. He wants to take our death and give us life, to take our sin and give us a Savior, to take our hell and give us heaven, to take our past and give us a future, and take our religion and give us relationship through the gift of salvation, granting new hearts and new desires. Our God says, *'…"You shall be holy, for I am holy."' (1 Peter 1:16)* God's word tells us that *'…the peace of God, which surpasses all understanding, will guard your hearts and your minds in Christ Jesus.' (Philippians 4:7)* He will give eyes and hearts for him through faith. Our faithful God will provide all who turn from their way and believe the good news with all we need to endure temptation and have forgiveness. And again, regarding the heart his word says, *'Keep your heart with all vigilance, for from it flow the springs of life.' (Proverbs 4:23)*

Jesus said, *"'…repent and believe in the gospel.'" (Mark 1:15)* God commands us to have a change of mind, turning from sin and to God, believing that Jesus paid for all our sins at the cross, died, and rose again, defeating death. He provides this repentance, faith, and forgiveness as a free gift and it is received by all who do not reject the truth. He is calling you with this good news. May we have new sight, by way of the cross, and may we look and live.

I am one who lusted with my eyes and flesh, and committed adultery with my eyes and heart, and God forgave me all of it and gave me a new life by filling me with the Holy Spirit. The word of God reveals *'...the fruit of the Spirit is love, joy, peace, patience, kindness, goodness, faithfulness, gentleness, self-control; against such things there is no law.' (Galatians 5:22-23)* I am not a perfect man but I can tell you he forgave and changed me when I looked to the perfect One who hung on the cross for sinners just like you and me. He sacrificially loves and lives, pouring out his steadfast love on every child he receives. The word of God says *'...if you confess with your mouth that Jesus is Lord and believe in your heart that God raised him from the dead, you will be saved.' (Romans 10:9)* May we have the wonderful heart knowledge of him, and receive the new sight, by faith, promised by him today.

6

....

Who's Thirsty?

'A woman from Samaria came to draw water. Jesus said to her, "Give me a drink." (For his disciples had gone away into the city to buy food.) The Samaritan woman said to him, "How is it that you, a Jew, ask for a drink from me, a woman of Samaria?" (For Jews have no dealings with Samaritans.) Jesus answered her, "If you knew the gift of God, and who it is that is saying to you, 'Give me a drink,' you would have asked him, and he would have given you living water." The woman said to him, "Sir, you have nothing to draw water with, and the well is deep. Where do you get that living water? Are you greater than our father Jacob? He gave us the well and drank from it himself, as did his sons and his livestock." Jesus said to her, "Everyone who drinks of this water will be thirsty again, but whoever drinks of the water that I will give him will never be thirsty again. The water that I will give him will become in him a spring of water welling up to eternal life." The woman said to him, "Sir, give me this water, so that I will not be thirsty or have to come here to draw water." Jesus said to her, "Go, call your husband, and come here." The woman answered him, "I have no husband." Jesus said to her, "You are right in saying, 'I have no husband';

for you have had five husbands, and the one you now have
is not your husband. What you have said is true.'"
(John 4:7-18)
-the word of God

Jesus, being fully God and yet fully man, is tired and wearied from his trip on foot and so he sits beside a well. A Samaritan woman is taken off guard and pretty much stunned with the request from Jesus for a drink. There was animosity between the Jews and the Samaritans at that time. The Jews looked down on the Samaritans as half-breeds. They lacked the pedigree. They just didn't measure up in the eyes of the Jews, not in ancestry, not in status, not in how they worshipped, or their understanding about God. You could imagine that this animosity was a two way street with the hatred of Jews by the Samaritan people as well. In that time it was also unheard of for a man to be asking a woman for pretty much anything. Jesus, breaking the cultural "rules" and biases, shows his love and intent with this request for a drink. He then says, '...*"If you knew the gift of God, and who it is that is saying to you, 'Give me a drink,' you would have asked him, and he would have given you living water.'"* (John 4:10)

The water that she was there to draw up was water that could only quench the thirst for a little while. But it couldn't satisfy the soul. Jesus was talking about a different kind of water, the kind that would satisfy for eternity, living water which is the Holy Spirit.

The Samaritan woman is confused by this exchange with Jesus. She sees this man who is unlike any Jew she has ever heard about, never mind talked to. He doesn't judge as the world judges. He is not condescending or hateful, but wants to give her the gift of God: the Holy Spirit, Living Water. She wonders who this man thinks he is, and doubts, questioning if Jesus is greater than their patriarch

Jacob who had passed on. Jesus responds to her, *"Everyone who drinks of this water will be thirsty again, but whoever drinks of the water that I will give him will never be thirsty again. The water that I will give him will become in him a spring of water welling up to eternal life."* *(John 4:13-14)*

Jesus is showing her, and us, what true thirst is and that it is only satisfied through him. It's a thirst that only he can fill, and it is a spiritual thirst. The Living Water that Jesus sends, seals believers souls for eternity, that we who believe may know we are heaven bound. This Living Water refreshes and renews. This Living Water gives fellowship with God and the knowledge of him and his will. This Living Water brings a transformation and new life in the person he fills. The Holy Spirit is always vibrant and alive in the one that he lives in. He proceeds from the Father and is sent by Jesus.

Jesus was willing and eager to freely send this Living Water, the Holy Spirit, to the Samaritan woman, and to all of us who believe. He shares his eagerness and willingness in another place in Scripture when he says, *"And I tell you, ask, and it will be given to you; seek, and you will find; knock, and it will be opened to you. For everyone who asks receives, and the one who seeks finds, and to the one who knocks it will be opened. What father among you, if his son asks for a fish, will instead of a fish give him a serpent; or if he asks for an egg, will give him a scorpion? If you then, who are evil, know how to give good gifts to your children, how much more will the heavenly Father give the Holy Spirit to those who ask him!"* *(Luke 11:9-13)*

It is God who is extending to us the good news of the gospel and showing us the result of receiving the gift of God. Jesus showed the woman that it is simply by asking for the Living Water; and again, how the Father will give the Holy Spirit to those who ask. Ask, seek, and knock. He is telling us to expect to receive, to find what you are looking for, and for a door to be opened for you, where you previously had no access! And call him Father because he loves all as his children who love him.

We see something awesome here. *The woman said to him, "Sir, give me this water, so that I will not be thirsty or have to come here to draw water." (John 4:15)* She obviously did not fully understand the depth of what Jesus was saying and the implications for eternity. But how did Jesus respond? He did not criticize her for not knowing where Living Water was in the Old Testament, or that Living Water was the Holy Spirit. He didn't shut her down as a half-breed nothing Samaritan, and a woman at that. He didn't disqualify her because she had doubted, and was still talking about the water from the well. Just like with any of us, he is not going to shut us down for maybe never having read the bible, or because we weren't much of church goers or that we lived however we pleased and are very sinful. He doesn't look to condemn us because our faith may have been superficial; even if we are church goers and claim to be Christians, while thinking by our own 'goodness' we could earn our way into heaven; when we learn that grace means something we don't deserve: favor that is unmerited. In place of the *superficial*, Jesus wants to make it *official* by sending the Holy Spirit.

He immediately begins to do with her as he does with all that he brings to saving faith. He shows the woman her sin and guilt, to bring her to repentance.

Jesus said to her, "Go, call your husband, and come here." The woman answered him, "I have no husband." Jesus said to her, "You are right in saying, 'I have no husband'; for you have had five husbands, and the one you now have is not your husband. What you have said is true."' (John 4:16-18) Because Jesus is God in the flesh he is omniscient so he knows everything we have ever done. He shows the woman her adultery, and her need for repentance, a changing of mind. It is something that he will do with us through conviction by the Holy

Spirit. God is bringing many to repentance, granting forgiveness of sins against Him, and faith in his Son who paid them in full with the shedding of his sinless blood on sinners' behalf on the cross so those who believe wouldn't have to pay. He is ready to send the Holy Spirit, filling those who receive with this Living Water so that we may have a new life in him and no longer live in the drought of spiritual thirst. The Triune God: Father, Son, and Holy Spirit, is ready to come and fill humbled hearts with the Living Water. He knows all we have ever done and still wants to rescue people from the condemnation of judgment for sinful unbelief, by his grace through faith. There is heaven and hell, two roads. One is known as the kingdom of God where all who enter will dwell for eternity and is filled with inexpressible joy and peace; the other is known as hell for eternal punishment of fire that does not cease, and he is drawing people to be with him in heaven. He is '...*not wishing that any should perish, but that all should reach repentance.' (2 Peter 3:9)* He is drawing people up to himself as from a well, even now. Jesus wants us to know where we are going, and give us the assurance today through faith, for all who believe, and calling all to repent.

'...*"If anyone thirsts, let him come to me and drink. Whoever believes in me, as the Scripture has said, 'Out of his heart will flow rivers of living water.'" Now this he said about the Spirit, whom those who believed in him were to receive, for as yet the Spirit had not been given, because Jesus was not yet glorified.' (John 7:37-39)* Jesus was glorified upon his resurrection on the third day from his death, and burial. He is alive and gives us good news. May God grant you a spiritual thirst that would be satisfied, even this very day, having faith in his Son, and a good conscience toward the Holy One.

(A godly saint, Kenneth Narvesen, shared a message that greatly influenced me, and God led me to share the gospel message above, to the glory of Christ. All praise to the holy name of Jesus!)

7

My Father?

Many of us are fearful of, or reject the notion of God because of personal biases with regard to our own dads. Perhaps it is that your father died when you were just a child. Maybe you had a father who ran off when you were young, or whose actions have torn your family apart. For some it may be that you had a father who was physically, emotionally, mentally, or sexually abusive. Or could it be that your father was very controlling: being critical and judgmental? It is quite possible that for some of you who are reading this your father brought you up with a different religion where God is not known as Father, or loving. Then we hear that God wants us to know him as our loving Father and we may be cynical. "Another father?"

Our experiences with our earthly fathers may distort our perception of who God is. Maybe our thoughts become so distorted that we become angry with God and try to suppress the truth about him, even saying he does not exist, accepting false theories of unbelieving men. But deep down we know we are lying and not telling the truth. We look at the wonder of creation and know this is not an accident or some random event. We look at children, we look at the stars, and at the world around us with all its complexity and know we have not been truthful, even with our own selves. Creation bears witness to the Creator.

Our God is awesome, holy, and good. He is a Father to the fatherless, and wants to know all who come to him as his child. He wants to shower those who believe in him with the love we never had from our fathers on earth, whether they were loving or not. The Father wants to forgive the times of anger towards him, which are our sins against him. He desires all who believe in Christ to know how very much they are loved and favored, by no good we have ever done, but by what he has done. God is not like a man for him to lie. He has proven his love by keeping his promises of prophecy and sending his Son Jesus, the Christ, to the earth to live the perfect life without sin; dying in place of sinners, and then raising him from the dead. He never lied, stole, looked with lust, blasphemed, hated, murdered, worshiped falsely, dishonored his Father, or did anything evil. He kept all the commandments of God and willingly took God's wrath for sin upon himself in place of sinful people. The word of God says, *'For Christ also suffered once for sins, the righteous for the unrighteous, that he might bring us to God, being put to death in the flesh but made alive in the spirit…' (1 Peter 3:18).* He did this in love that all who believe would be forgiven and become children of God.

And why would God do that? Jesus tells us, *"For God so loved the world, that he gave his only Son, that whoever believes in him should not perish but have eternal life." (John 3:16)* God loves the ones that earthly fathers neglected and mistreated. God loves those who love him. Every sin was laid on Jesus, God in the flesh, that all who believe may be forgiven and brought into God's family and kingdom of heaven, instead of his just judgment of hell. God punished his Son Jesus in place of sinners: that by faith we could go free. God will take your unrighteousness and grant you the righteousness of Jesus Christ if you turn from your way, confess Jesus, and have saving faith in his resurrection from the dead. God will bring you into a relationship with him through faith in his Son.

God is calling you to repentance. We have sinned against God and he is calling us to lay it all down, to change our mind about what we have done and believe that Jesus Christ paid for every sin in our lives, by dying for them, and then rising from the dead. He paid the penalty that all who believe would become children of God and know him as Father. God is calling, and can save those who seem to be the most distant from him. He is calling the far away and afraid and in need of spiritual healing from their Holy Father. What is the Father like? Look at Jesus to know, and hear him say, *"'I and the Father are one.'" (John 10:30)*

God is a defender and deliverer of the fatherless. This Holy God is also known as the God of love. He extends the message of forgiveness and salvation through faith, providing his children with the promise of his everlasting love and gift of eternal life, and that he would never leave or forsake, like some earthly fathers who have walked out on their children. He is calling you. The Father is calling us to know him through his Son. Jesus, the Son of God, said, *"But the hour is coming, and is now here, when the true worshipers will worship the Father in spirit and truth, for the Father is seeking such people to worship him. God is spirit, and those who worship him must worship in spirit and truth.'" (John 4:23-24)* He does this because of his very own righteousness and love. Let us no longer be lost, but be found by this great and only God who wants all who believe to be known as his beloved children, and for them to know him as Abba, which means Father.

8

....

Who is God?

What does Holy Scripture tell us about who God is, and what kind of worship is pure, pleasing, and acceptable to him?

Jesus tells us,

> *"God is spirit, and those who worship him must worship in spirit and truth."* *(John 4:24)*

What does Scripture tell us about Jesus? Who is he?

> *'He is the image of the invisible God...'* *(Colossians 1:15)*

Jesus also said,

> *"I and the Father are one."* *(John 10:30)*

Without Jesus we cannot know God the Father, for he has made himself known through Jesus, his Son. If we do not believe God's word conveyed to us, or attempt to read it for ourselves, how would we know what he reveals about himself, and what is acceptable and truthful worship?

Who is God? If Jesus is anything less than God to you, then you do not know God, for God is One. He has made himself known through Christ, the sinless, crucified, risen and living Savior. Through faith in him is the only way to have forgiveness of sins, peace with God, and eternal life. *"And there is salvation in no one else, for there is no other name under heaven given among men by which we must be saved."* *(Acts 4:12)* So I ask you, do you know him?

9

··

It is Written

'as it is written:
"None is righteous, no, not one; no one understands; no
one seeks for God. All have turned aside; together they have
become worthless; no one does good, not even one." "Their
throat is an open grave; they use their tongues to deceive."
"The venom of asps is under their lips." "Their mouth is full
of curses and bitterness." "Their feet are swift to shed blood;
in their paths are ruin and misery, and the way of peace they
have not known." "There is no fear of God before their eyes."
Now we know that whatever the law says it speaks to those
who are under the law, so that every mouth may be stopped,
and the whole world may be held accountable to God."'
(Romans 3:10-19)
-the word of God

Our attempts at good works cannot save us, for holy God hates sin,
and cannot be bought with the bribe of our self-serving attempts to
please him in accordance to our own value system and efforts, or
our practicing of religion, no matter how good we or others think
of them. All our righteous deeds are but filthy rags to Holy God, so

what we consider good on the scales of man, carry no weight with God, and because of our sinfulness '...*it is appointed for man to die once, and after that comes judgment...*' *(Hebrews 9:27)*.

God requires payment to be made for sin, our offenses against the Almighty, and '...*the wages of sin is death...*' *(Romans 6:23)*. The decree of judgment is an eternity in hell. Jesus called it a place of '... *unquenchable fire*' *(Mark 9:43)*, where there will be '...*weeping and gnashing of teeth...*' *(Luke 13:28)*. Our blood be on our own heads! But God who is just in sending us to hell also provided the way of escape and forgiveness. He has a love far greater than ours, and mercy that is unmatched, for he alone is good. God has sacrificial love, and provided a blood sacrifice in place of sinners. But what sacrifice can break the curse of sin? What can deliver from death and judgment, and the flames and torment of hell?

God's ways are higher than ours, and his ways unfathomable. For someone who has not even considered it truthfully may deem it impossible, or even untrue, especially through indoctrination of multiple ways to the contrary. But those who discount God's way will not be saved, but will suffer torment for all eternity for their sins against holy God. Truly, it would be better to have never been born than to go there.

But this good God did deliver, and by his own might, for he is also known as Redeemer. God, the Almighty, humbled himself. The great and only God, who transcends time and space, came to the earth by his eternal Spirit, becoming fully man as well, in the person of Jesus. God was in heaven and at the same time walked among his creation on earth as a man. He did what sinful man could not. He kept the Law of God, all God's commandments, and did so perfectly. He lived a pure and holy life, and did it among temptations of all kinds, without giving in once, '...*for God cannot be tempted with evil...*' *(James 1:13)*.

He lived and did good, real good, unlike our self-righteous rags. He healed all who were sick and oppressed by the devil. He fed thousands well, with a small meal, and performed many miracles, showing himself to be God. Nothing was difficult for him, and he did all things perfectly, for what is hard or impossible for the One who set the stars in their place, and designed each person to his pleasing? Who are we to tell the glorious One how he can reveal himself, or where he can be, and where he cannot? God takes council with himself, and we are but his creation. He is far higher in thought, and power is his alone. He reveals himself, yet many cannot fathom it. He shows himself through the things he has made in creation, and we are baffled by it, even with many who try to explain it away. He proclaims his will, and it is done. He prophesies it, telling us beforehand that it will be, and who can keep his word from being fulfilled?

God's word says, *'For my thoughts are not your thoughts, neither are your ways my ways, declares the Lord. For as the heavens are higher than the earth, so are my ways higher than your ways and my thoughts than your thoughts.' (Isaiah 55:8-9)*

Jesus loved all, revealing who God is and what he is like. Jesus was pure and holy, revealing the great God who dwells in magnificent and unapproachable light. Jesus taught with authority, and the religious hypocrites were confounded. Jesus proclaimed his death, burial, and resurrection, and thought of all the great amount of people that he would pay the penalty for and bring to salvation, as he willingly went to the cross to be crucified.

God's design required a holy sacrifice, as a choice lamb without spot or blemish. That is why Jesus is called the Lamb of God, for he is the One without the blemish and spots of sin and unrighteousness that make the sacrifice deemed unworthy. It had to be Jesus, God making the sacrifice for man himself, becoming a living sacrifice;

the payment fully pleasing and acceptable to God. God, Holy God, loves to save sinners, for there are none righteous, no, not even one, *'as it is written…' (Romans 3:10).*

God came to destroy the works of the devil in the person of the Messiah, the Anointed One, and came with the good news of himself, revealing his righteousness, salvation by faith through Jesus Christ. God continues to reach down for sinful man through the message of the cross, and shows there is power in the blood of Jesus, to save and provide a new life through his Spirit that is holy. He shows his perfection, and his covenant with himself, that he would save. Do you know Jesus, the truth about the Righteous One? Do you know your Creator and God who loves?

Jesus was hated by the unrighteous and went as was prophesied about him. According to God's incorruptible word, Jesus was treated with contempt, despised by many, pierced through his hands and feet, and made the ultimate sacrifice for our sin. Blood ran from his head, due to the sharp crown of thorns savagely placed, his back was laid open from the brutal lashes of scourging, and holy blood poured out of his human body as he was in the anguish of physical pain, yet fully God as he prayed for sinners, even for those who pierced and mocked him as he hung on the cross, praying, *'…"Father, forgive them, for they know not what they do.".…' (Luke 23:34)* Finally, from the cross, at the fulfillment of his mission, signifying his perfect sacrifice pleasing to God the Father, he said, *'…"It is finished!" And he bowed his head and gave up his spirit.' (John 19:30)*

He died. God the Father was glorified with the sacrifice of his only Son, the Lord Jesus, through his life and through his death; but death could not hold him. Death could not stop the Author of Life. Speaking of his life before going to the cross, Jesus said, *'"No one takes it from me, but I lay it down of my own accord. I have authority to lay it down, and I have authority to take it up again."' (John 10:18)* God is Spirit, and though the body laid dead the Spirit never ceased, for God cannot stop being God. On the third day, after being enclosed in a stone tomb, an angel was sent to roll away the large stone, his Spirit returned, and Jesus, in glorified and imperishable body, came forth. He was and is alive, and says '…"Come."…' *(Revelation 22:17)*

His message is the same today as yesterday, and has not changed in two thousand years: '…*repent and believe in the gospel.*' *(Mark 1:15)* Change your mind, and believe the good news from heaven about Jesus, that you may receive forgiveness of sins in his name, and a new life from God.

Following 40 days of time spent with his disciples, showing himself to over 500 of them at one time in his glorified and resurrected body, after speaking about the kingdom of God, Jesus ascended back to heaven. But he did not, nor does he ever leave his true followers alone. God sends the Holy Spirit, down to this very day. It is God, the transcendent, the One who will not be held by human precepts or religions of men, who is the ever-present One. And he is also the same One God, who dwells in heaven, and sends his followers of himself. He fills the heart of every person that he brings to saving faith, sealing them as his own children, by his Holy Spirit, showing that they are his, as family, who live, and who love, and are set apart and made holy by his Spirit.

God is pleased for his beloved children to call him Holy Father, and Jesus, who is God in resurrected and eternal body, is pleased to call his followers brothers, and God, the Holy Spirit, shows his love for his family by coming to live within them in Spirit and truth, having the righteousness of Jesus Christ counted to them, directing the followers actions and thoughts in accordance to God's will in what is good, cleansing by faith.

There are not three gods, but One, who reveals himself as Father, Son, Holy Spirit. His ways are truly not our ways, they are far better. God's ways may be unfathomable, but they are best. God's ways may confuse and shock, but his way is the only way. Jesus said, *"'Come to me, all who labor and are heavy laden, and I will give you rest.'" (Matthew 11:28)* Through a change of mind and faith, you can receive forgiveness from God, and a whole new life that pleases him. God wants fellowship by Spirit, in love, with his worshipers, and seeks unity and a family relationship among all believers, and that is found exclusively through Jesus.

There is only One God, and all will bow to him. Eternal life and unmerited favor await those who receive his immeasurable and undeserved gift. He extends good news to you, as written, and will send his pure and Holy Spirit to all who believe, God coming to live inside, not because we are good, but because he is, and only those who share in his Spirit know God, and belong to him. May you receive him and know his holy and sacrificial love this very day.

10

··

Three Criminals

'As many were astonished at you—
his appearance was so marred, beyond human semblance,
and his form beyond that of the children of mankind—'
(Isaiah 52:14)
-the word of God

I shared a meal with a fellow believer in Christ a few months back. We got into studying the end of the book of the prophet Isaiah, chapter 52, and into Isaiah chapter 53, the prophecies that were over 700 years before Christ came down from heaven to earth, to be born of a virgin, through the Holy Spirit. We shared about how much Jesus endured and how disfigured and unhuman he looked from the violence and merciless scourging he received from the hatred of wicked and sinful men. It is overwhelming that Jesus, my God and Creator, my King, would hang naked and bloodied like pulp, in raw flesh, with skin no longer hanging, but sloughed off.

He hung there, held up with spikes through his hands and feet in love for me. All my sins were laid on him and Jesus Christ suffered in my place. He took all the wrath of God, against himself that day. It should have been three criminals hanging there, and though completely innocent he hung there instead of me, crucified amongst two criminals, one at his right hand and one at his left, to save me. Even some of the Roman soldiers must have been sick to see Jesus crucified in this way, for no one has ever been scourged and beaten and abused ever like this before, or ever will again.

It was a bloodbath, a pool of blood that flowed from the body of my precious Savior, the Son of God who is God. Poured out for sinners, was his blood, paying the price for sin, and to tear the dividing line that sin causes, that separates us from God. Look at what it cost him to save sinners like us. Is that a man up there? Look how ugly our sin is, and what it cost him to save all who would believe. My God and my King! All my wretched sins have been laid on Jesus. He took the wrath of holy God, God saving through faith by taking the punishment upon himself, by crushing his Son. He did it for sinners just like me. Believe that you may know that he did it for you too!

If you have never trusted in Jesus Christ, turn from your sins, and believe in the *only* God who loved so much so as to take the punishment and place of many. Believe on the One who shed his blood, died, and rose from the dead after three days. '...*"Believe in the Lord Jesus, and you will be saved..."' (Acts 16:31).*

11

···

Humbled or Haughty

'You save a humble people, but your eyes are
on the haughty to bring them down.'
(2 Samuel 22:28)
-the word of God

To become proud, being high, lifted and raised in one's own estimations of self, is what being haughty is. God hates the sin of pride, for it is the sin of Satan. It is demonic, and at enmity with God. The one who is haughty is thinking more of oneself than should, and elevating him or herself, but God reveals this to us for good reason.

There is no one who has ever approached God and has been restored to the Lord while being proud or boastful. Only the humbled are saved, and that by God's grace. I was a prideful and arrogant man: haughty. Thank God he humbled me under his mighty hand of mercy and grace, and that he saved and changed me through his unmerited favor, granting me a whole new life. He brought me low to lift me up from my sinful and high minded state. Indeed, *'Pride goes before destruction, and a haughty spirit before a fall.'* *(Proverbs 16:18)* And also, *'Before destruction a man's heart is haughty, but humility comes before honor.' (Proverbs 18:12)*

The haughty person has no room for a real relationship with God, for that person's heart is too full of self, and swollen with conceit. We all have done what is right in our own sight, but how God sees us is most important, and his ways are best. For, *'There is a way that seems right to a man, but its end is the way to death.' (Proverbs 16:25)*

Thank God he does not want this death for us, for having a haughty spirit brings destruction, yet those humbled through repentance by heeding his reproof and believing the good news of the gospel are filled with his Holy Spirit. God sent Jesus Christ to the earth, God who took on human form, to live the sinless life, being fully man. He was fully God, creation being created through him, yet he humbled himself to come and serve a condemned world with his very life, even humbling himself to be treated with hatred by mankind, up to and including his very death on the cross.

He came for sinners, including the proud and boastful, and took their sins upon himself by becoming a holy sacrifice that would meet God's demands for payment of sin, by taking every haughty act upon himself; all the pride, every arrogant act, and condescending thing ever done to another, that all who would believe on his Son would be saved. Believe that Jesus shed his blood for all of it, and you can be forgiven because he died in your place, and rose again from death. He provides this forgiveness, faith, and transformation; a gift of unmerited favor. He fills with the Holy Spirit, and provides new life, filled with a change of heart that produces, by his Spirit, precious *'...love, joy, peace, patience, kindness, goodness, faithfulness, gentleness, self-control; against such things there is no law.' (Galatians 5:22-23)* No command of condemnation to hell for sin is counted to these. This is received by a change of mind and faith in the Lord Jesus.

When asked about what is the greatest commandment, Jesus proclaimed, *'..."You shall love the Lord your God with all your heart* and with all your soul and with all your mind. *This is the great and first commandment. And a second is like it: You shall love your neighbor as yourself." (Matthew 22:37-39)* This love is found in the humbled and believing, with the Holy Spirit.

The evidence that this has happened is the transformed life that hungers and thirsts for God's righteousness. It is not something that those who remain proud can receive. It is not received by the self-righteous who remain haughty, being high in their estimations, as though they could earn salvation, for the gift of God is unmerited, for he saves sinners and provides salvation from his very own love and favor, as a gift. He saves them from the condemnation of hell where all sinners go without grace. Do you know Jesus? God doesn't want you to go there. Do you have his Spirit within you? Are you sure, or are you being high minded? Religious pride keeps as many people from God, who have trusted in their church doctrines, and performance, and not in what God has revealed in his holy word. Sadly, there will be many in hell like these.

'Thus says the Lord: "Let not the wise man boast in his wisdom, let not the mighty man boast in his might, let not the rich man boast in his riches, but let him who boasts boast in this, that he understands and knows me, that I am the Lord who practices steadfast love, justice, and righteousness in the earth. For in these things I delight, declares the Lord."' (Jeremiah 9:23-24)

May we all be brought to a change of mind about sin through repentance and faith that Jesus has paid for our sins in full through his sacrificial love by bearing our sins upon himself, taking the full punishment and wrath due your sins and mine. May we not wait for tomorrow to be reconciled to God and remain proud, for tomorrow is not promised. And may those of us who know the Lord steer clear of thinking more highly of ourselves for what God is doing in us, for God opposes it within his followers as well.

May we not reject the good news of God when it is before us. Let us be reconciled to him this day, for ...*"God opposes the proud, but gives grace to the humble."* *(James 4:6)* Truly the humbled are blessed and granted eternal life, with no condemnation, and lifted high to holy heaven, for those who know Jesus. My prayer is that you would be too. Jesus is the *only* One *highly* exalted and above *all* others. Do you know him? '...*"Let the one who boasts, boast in the Lord."'* *(1 Corinthians 1:31)*

12

....

Earthly or Heavenly Treasure

*"'No one can serve two masters, for either he will hate the
one and love the other, or he will be devoted to the one and
despise the other. You cannot serve God and money.'"*
(Matthew 6:24)
-Jesus Christ the Righteous

Here is a question to my friends who love money. Whom do you
serve? What or who do you talk about the most? If you love God you
would talk about him. But if you love money you would talk about
your funds, or your pursuit of it. If you love God you will worship
Jesus. If you love money then you will worship it.

One more question for the ones who love money. It's a
question that Jesus asked. *"For what will it profit a man if he
gains the whole world and forfeits his soul? Or what shall a man
give in return for his soul?"' (Matthew 16:26)* You may love your
money and your possessions, but it will never satisfy, and will
never deliver or save your soul. Your money cannot deliver you
from death, or even purchase your soul more time than what
God has predetermined for it on this earth. Having money is
not bad, but *'...the love of money is a root of all kinds of evils...' (1*

Timothy 6:10). It is an idol in the life of the lover of it, and leads to more evil.

The life of love for money is idolatry, as bowing down before a statue of some sort, and is certainly spiritually poor. It is sin, and *'...the wages of sin is death...' (Romans 6:23).* There is a judgment coming after death when we see God, and the judgment is eternal torment in hell for those who remain in sin. How will the lovers of money fare with their Creator whom they hate and despise, loving what God has given rather than the Giver of life, salvation, and all provision?

Thank God that he loves sinners, and that he came down to the earth as Jesus, to live the sinless life and to make the ultimate sacrifice that all who believe may be saved. Jesus calls all people to repent and believe in the gospel. The Holy One, the great God and Savior, was crucified by those who hated him, but according to the perfect plan of God, so as to take the place of sinners, that we who believe may live.

Jesus rose from the dead and is the living Savior of all who live by faith. He is the true treasure of every believer, and those who believe are rich in him. Jesus said, *"Do not lay up for yourselves treasures on earth, where moth and rust destroy and where thieves break in and steal, but lay up for yourselves treasures in heaven, where neither moth nor rust destroys and where thieves do not break in and steal. For where your treasure is, there your heart will be also." (Matthew 6:19-21)* Real treasure is not green but blood red, loving us by shedding it to cleanse us from our sins and providing faith that we may forsake our way and live.

Jesus, the One who came from heaven and ascended back to heaven is calling you to repent, to change your mind about sin and toward God, and to believe the gospel, the good news about his sacrifice for sinners. Believe in the One who can forgive your idolatry and grant you a whole new life. Believe in the One who can make the spiritually poor into spiritually rich in God. Believe on the risen Lord Jesus Christ, more precious than all silver and gold, and you will be saved.

13

....

Belief in Unbelief

I have atheist friends that proudly say they do not believe in God. They may appear confident in their assertions, but their hearts are exposed by their very own beliefs and by the word of God. They say that God does not exist, though the word of truth bears witness about those who say so, and a root of the problem. *'In the pride of his face the wicked does not seek him; all his thoughts are, "There is no God."' (Psalm 10:4)* Indeed, all mankind has done wicked things, but non who have ever come to saving faith in their Creator have ever did so while being proud, but only in humility.

Atheists have eerily made their very hope the grave, that they might live their life in the fashion that pleases their sinful passions; that they will not have to face the judgment of God for their deeds, hoping their death will be the end. Holy Scripture teaches that they suppress the truth in unrighteousness, and deny it, worshiping the creature, themselves or other created things, rather than the Creator, so that they may attempt self-deception, numbing their consciences from the truth about God that is so very evident within them. Many look at the intricate creation and try to deny the witness of it, though all around and in every place, it testifies, "Made by the

Creator." Indeed, *'The heavens declare the glory of God, and the sky above proclaims his handiwork.' (Psalm 19:1)*

Many are extreme in their views, and will seek opportunities to attack truth with error, jumping from subject to subject in their arsenal of, "Did God really say?" Their mantra is their lie of belief in unbelief, no matter how much they proclaim and repeat their hatred towards him by doing so, will in no way lessen the absolute fact of their day in the courtroom of this holy God of righteousness and truth. Jesus said, *"'I tell you, on the day of judgment people will give account for every careless word they speak, for by your words you will be justified, and by your words you will be condemned.'"* *(Matthew 12:36-37)*

Our very fingertips bear witness, how uniquely we are made by God, and in his image. We have one-of-a-kind fingerprints, with no two people having the same, even distinct among identical twins, showing the workmanship of God who made us, his imprint upon us from the God who is one-of-a-kind as well, for God is One. To deny our Creator, we not only have to suppress the truth that is within us, but also to suppress the truth that has been stamped upon us. We cannot so much as use our hands without it bearing witness, even if we use them unrighteously to say different, as with the culmination of pen or keyboard strokes with our digits to spread our unbelief, and attempt to attack the truth. Will we also deny these fingers as well?

Atheists put their hope in flawed theory rather than fact, and hold tightly to it, though believing in myth and bad science rather than biblical fact and truth. They shake their fists at the omnipotent and merciful God who continues to give them breath, in his kindness, restraint, and mercy, as they exhale hate and blasphemy toward him to whom they will one day give an account. Indeed, *'The fool says in his heart, "There is no God.".....' (Psalm 14:1)*

Though this may seem harsh to some, it is far from it. *'For we ourselves were once foolish, disobedient, led astray, slaves to various passions and pleasures, passing our days in malice and envy, hated by others and hating one another.' (Titus 3:3)* We have all fallen short of the glory of God. I love atheists very much, and earnestly seek their salvation, to know the awesome Savior who saved me, granting me forgiveness and a new life. The truth of the word of God has great benefit for what it reveals about us, that we may see ourselves truthfully as God sees us, that we may turn from our way and live. The word of God reveals to us that God's kindness, forbearance, and patience is meant to lead us to repentance. It is out of love that God shines light on our thinking and intentions, and sends the good news of the gospel for all people, that we may know his awesome power for salvation, for he is calling a people out of this world, granting the gift of faith, by grace. Can atheists be saved? Of course they can, and the same way all others are, through believing the gospel, by grace.

This awesome Creator came to rescue us, his creation, from our sinfulness and flawed thinking. He came to be light in this world of spiritual darkness. Our Lord also came to save those who have shaken their fists at this good God, to humble and bring near those who have denied him in their hearts, and wrongly tried justifying their unbelief in a good God by the evil and disease that is in this fallen world due to sin.

He is the God of compassion and mercy, who is not like us, but infinitely better, and so did what we could never do. God sent his eternal Son, the fully Divine who also became fully man by coming from heaven to earth, to be born by miracle birth. He humbled himself, and came to serve his creation, two thousand years ago, with his awesome love and goodness of this gospel message of himself, that extends all the way to this very day, both to you and me. The One without sin, though tempted in every way, took the predetermined and torturous road of suffering, though completely innocent, being falsely accused, mocked, and treated with contempt by people he showed his godly love to. He was brutally scourged with whips affixed with sharp pieces of materials to cause horrible amounts of bodily damage and removal of flesh, and then forced to carry his cross, dragging it as he left a trail of his righteous red blood to the destination of his crucifixion, as many followed and mocked with blood lust, while others wailed. He was brutally nailed to the pieces of the tree that he carried as his cross, through his hands and feet, and was lifted up to hang, from where he prayed to the Father as he hung between heaven and earth, who sent him for that very hour, to finish his course on his rescue mission. He prayed for the people who did this to him, though he willingly went to the cross, not only for the people who were among the crowds, but for sinners from all cultural groups, languages, nations, and beliefs down to this very day. He did it for those who live in ways far from him, to bring them near. He died in place of sins of all kinds, to save people through a change of mind toward God and faith in his Son, the One who rose from the dead after three days, and is very much alive. He sends his people to serve you with this good news of salvation that you may turn from unbelief and believe, having life in the name of Jesus. This is the message of hope, forgiveness, promise, and peace. May we receive this awesome news of salvation and the warning of the Holy Spirit when he says to us, '..."Today, if you hear His voice, do not harden your hearts..."' (Hebrews 3:7-8).

God is good, and holy, and it is he who brings salvation and who will one day judge the people of the whole world. How will you be found in that day? May we know him and hear his word that says to us, '...Behold, now is the favorable time; behold, now is the day of salvation.' (2 Corinthians 6:2) My hope and earnest prayer is that you will be found in Christ, and even this very day.

14

Not the Righteous, Only Sinners

"'I have not come to call the righteous but sinners to repentance.'"
(Luke 5:32)
-Jesus Christ the Righteous

When Jesus said this the religious leaders at that time, known as the Pharisees and the scribes, were grumbling against Jesus and his disciples for sharing a meal with those whom they looked down upon and condemned, as despised thieves and sinners of one kind or another. But what was the response of Jesus to them? *"I have not come to call the righteous but sinners to repentance.'" (Luke 5:32)*

What did that mean? Did that mean that the Pharisees and scribes were righteous? Did that mean that he was only calling people to repent that were really horrible sinners, and that righteous people were in the clear? No: not at all. Jesus was in effect saying that there are none righteous but only sinners. He also was in effect saying, 'I am not here for those who think they are righteous, but for those who know they are unrighteous.' He was in fact telling us that he is not coming for those who are inflated in their egos, believing in their self-righteousness and belief that they are good on their own and need no Jesus for their lives, but calling out and saving the ones that come face to face with their sinfulness and need of the Savior. Until we are humbled by God and brought to the point of recognizing our sinfulness, we will not hear his call to repentance and saving faith as something we need. The thinking for the Pharisee and scribe was that they were better than that, and righteous in themselves. They pointed out the sins of others, but rejected the fact that they were sinners themselves.

Jesus calls all sinners to repentance. Great news for you and me! He calls the drunks, liars, thieves, prostitutes, adulterers, the angry, the hateful, and all the other types of labels for our sinfulness; the very ones that the religious hypocrites of our day look down upon because they think they are better and try to do good by their own standard of self-righteousness. He calls those that the world may look down upon by their lofty standards of hypocrisy. He calls the broken and forgotten by the elitists of this world who mock and ridicule. The Savior calls men and women who are bowed down in the anguish of the reality of their sinfulness, and brings them to repentance, a change of mind, and faith in the Lord Jesus Christ, and all by his power and grace. He calls his people to go out into the world and to do the same, extending good news to all people, no matter what they label themselves, or what labels others have called them.

He is still calling and granting eternal life and escape from the judgment of hell, not to those who stay in their self-righteousness, but to those who are brought to know they are sinners. He calls people, even this day, to repentance and faith in him. He, the Lord Jesus, the One whom God created the heavens and the earth through, the sinless Lord and Savior of the world, is calling sinners to repent and believe in his sacrificial death for them and his resurrection from the dead, clothing all who come to him with his righteousness, and all by the unmerited favor of God. It is extended to those who do not deserve it, and by doing so transforming their lives to the glory of God. And yes, he calls the prideful who he humbles to see their unrighteous sinfulness and need of a Savior. What good news and great love from God. May we have ears to hear his call.

15

....

From Darkness to Light

Many people are intrigued with psychics, mediums, tarot cards, angel cards, palm reading, fortune telling, witchcraft, shamanism, the occult, reiki, false worship in yoga, and things like these. I used to be one of them in the sense that I played with the aouija board and was exposed to many strange things in my younger years. Some of us already know that there is something else out there beyond what we can see with the human eye. We may think it is a big game or of great insight, but what we may not know or have accepted readily enough is that it is done by satanic power and whoever does these things is flirting with the devil. Some think it is entertainment, like going to a psychic during a bachelorette party, or for others it may be going to seek a medium to communicate with a dead loved one that may be mourned for. But what does the word of God say? *"Do not turn to mediums or necromancers; do not seek them out, and so make yourselves unclean by them: I am the LORD your God."' (Leviticus 19:31)*

God abhors evil for he is holy, and knows that your communication and turning to these people are actually opening you up to demons. Satan is known as the father of all lies. He is a master deceiver and can even disguise himself as an angel of light, sort of like a wolf in sheep's clothing. He would love to have you trusting in him and his deceptions, to tangle a web around you and catch you in it. He longs to surround you with sorcery and captivate your mind with delusions. The medium or psychic may tell you something about a loved one who has passed on with complete accuracy, which only the two of you, you and your deceased loved one would have known. But the devil knows about the two of you as well. There are many fallen angels we know by the term of demons. What we fail to realize is that Satan is a clever devil and looks to keep you from God, and the devil would love to torment your soul.

There was a lot of witchcraft and satanic activity from long ago. That is why God has said in his word, *"'There shall not be found among you anyone who burns his son or his daughter as an offering, anyone who practices divination or tells fortunes or interprets omens, or a sorcerer or a charmer or a medium or a necromancer or one who inquires of the dead, for whoever does these things is an abomination to the LORD...'" (Deuteronomy 18:10-12).*

Now we may not see or hear of people sacrificing their children as a burnt offering to a false god (demon) as they did long ago, with exception to occultic type practices, but we do hear of these other practices in this day and age. It has been around since sin has, and seems to be growing all the more. Why is this important? If you haven't noticed this is very serious in the sight of Holy God who is the Righteous Judge, and who sees these practices as defiling to a person and an abomination to the person practicing and receiving such things.

The word of God says, *'...should not a people inquire of their God? Should they inquire of the dead on behalf of the living?' (Isaiah 8:19)* And yet many have chased after Satan and death with open arms to his works of sin. In the book of 1ˢᵗ John it says, *'Whoever makes a practice of sinning is of the devil, for the devil has been sinning from the beginning. The reason the Son of God appeared was to destroy the works of the devil.' (1 John 3:8)*

There is a battle for your soul by the devil, to blind you and keep you in the dark, *'...to keep them from seeing the light of the gospel of the glory of Christ, who is the image of God.' (2 Corinthians 4:4)* You by no way can avail yourself, and have accepted what you know to be evil. Others are quite pleased with their new found spiritual life, and find it exhilarating and fun. You may not even realize it but you may be possessed by a demon, or demons, for playing with the works of the devil. Witchcraft can come in the form of drugs, spells, magic, false worship, idolatry, rebellion against holy God, and a willing acceptance to what is false. You need to be set free but no amount of medication, psychologists, self-help or will-power will do. Your only hope is in Jesus.

Why is Jesus the only hope? Jesus, the One whom God created us through, tells us why. *"For God so loved the world, that he gave his only Son, that whoever believes in him should not perish but have eternal life. For God did not send his Son into the world to condemn the world, but in order that the world might be saved through him. Whoever believes in him is not condemned, but whoever does not believe is condemned already, because he has not believed in the name of the only Son of God. And this is the judgment: the light has come into the world, and people loved the darkness rather than the light because their works were evil. For everyone who does wicked things hates the light and does not come to the light, lest his works should be exposed. But whoever does what is true comes to the light, so that it may be clearly seen that his works have been carried out in God."' (John 3:16-21)*

Come to the Light! God loves you, and can save you from facing judgment for your witchcraft and demonic practices. The judgment God has set forth for the works of sin is everlasting torment in the *'...eternal fire prepared for the devil and his angels.'*

(Matthew 25:41) God sent his holy Son to the earth to live the perfect life in the place of sinful people and he did so without sin, a holy life all of his life. Unlike you and me, Jesus was good and pure in every thought, word, and deed, completely set apart from darkness. While he walked the earth he cast out thousands of demons from the demon possessed and forgave sin. He taught of the kingdom of heaven and at God's appointed time he willingly became a living sacrifice, by shedding his pure blood and dying for sinners' uncleanness and abominations. God's wrath was poured out on his Son for every witchcraft, demonic conversation, attempt to communicate with the dead, fortune telling, sorcery, false worship, and every other evil sin of darkness and work of the devil, to bring his people from darkness to light. Then after three days Jesus rose from the dead, triumphant, forever defeating the power of sin and death for all who would believe. He ascended back to heaven and will return again for his followers, and to judge the world in perfect righteousness.

Jesus calls all to repent, to change their mind about sin and toward God, believing in the good news of the gospel that Jesus died for our sins that we may be forgiven and cleansed from all our unrighteousness, and grants a new life for all who call upon his name in truth. If you believe in Jesus, God will remove the uncleanness and abominations of darkness from your life, for he is the Light, and will count his perfect life to you, that God may see the blood of Jesus and not your own. Through faith, God would look at you as without sin, because of what Jesus has done for you on the cross. It is God's undeserved gift and amazing love for all who believe.

God can remove the evil spirit within the unclean and fill them with the Holy Spirit. You can have your blood cleansed by the holy blood of Jesus. You can know the true and all powerful Holy God and Father, who has the power to crush the works of Satan, and set you free from the power of sin, in the name of his Son. Jesus is still casting out demons and destroying the works of the devil. Leave the works of darkness, turn from sin, and come to the Light! Escape the clutches of hell and be heaven bound. The word of God says, *'if you confess with your mouth that Jesus is Lord and believe in your heart that God raised him from the dead, you will be saved.' (Romans 10:9)*

16

No More Namaste

'...And behold, the Lord passed by, and a great and strong
wind tore the mountains and broke in pieces the rocks before the
Lord, but the Lord was not in the wind. And after the wind an
earthquake, but the Lord was not in the earthquake. And after
the earthquake a fire, but the Lord was not in the fire...'
(1 Kings 19:11-12).
-the word of God

There are people who believe that God's essence is in everything.
They connect the creation to the Creator, yet make no distinction
between the two, as though they are one. But what does Scripture
teach us? The word of God shows us that God was not the wind,
but the cause of it. He sent such a strong wind that it tore the
mountains he created, and broke apart the rocks as they fell and
were scattered; yet he was not the mountains, nor the rocks he
made to break. Though God caused the earth to quake, being the
Almighty God, he showed that he was not the earth of which he
has full control, to cause it to be steady, or to shake. He too brought
forth a fire, but he was not in the fire that can most certainly be used
to light, heat, melt, and burn: being helpful, or to bring disaster. The

transcendent and Mighty God that cannot be held by his creation, that he most awesomely designed, has power over it, manifesting his omnipotence within our midst, causing us to be in awe. Yet he is not within these things at all.

There are beliefs that god is in everyone, that the universe is god, and also that we are the universe. Take your pick. But will we believe that which is contrary to what God reveals to us in his holy word? Our God is One and will not let you make him what you will, nor will he hear your prayer that is made falsely through the sin of pagan worship. Indeed, *'…your iniquities have made a separation between you and your God, and your sins have hidden his face from you so that he does not hear.' (Isaiah 59:2)*

Many believe in practicing yoga, a Hindu polytheistic philosophy which has techniques for breathing, movements, and stretching, where poses done and held are meant to represent and worship false gods, of which Hinduism has millions. This, which is passed off as innocent, is false worship that is actually being received by demons which are fallen angels who are evil, the enemies of the One true and Holy God. The word of truth says, *'…You cannot partake of the table of the Lord and the table of demons. Shall we provoke the Lord to jealousy? Are we stronger than he?' (1 Corinthians 10:21-22)* The Lord cares for his people, and will not share them with practices that are false and are in worship of demons. The Creator is not eclectic, and will not accept your worship, along with worship of any other spirit, for there is no God but One, and if we are truly his, we will turn away from practices that are false, and most certainly will not worship another, for that would be as having a divided heart. What would you think of a wife who cheated on a devout and loving husband? And will we think we can dabble with these practices from pagan faiths when we hear the word of truth, and follow Christ as well, or will we worship God with our whole heart?

The word of life says '...*what partnership has righteousness with lawlessness? Or what fellowship has light with darkness? What accord has Christ with Belial? Or what portion does a believer share with an unbeliever? What agreement has the temple of God with idols? For we are the temple of the living God...*' *(2 Corinthians 6:14-16)* providing we have repented from our sins, and believed that Christ died for sinners upon the cross. Who wants any accord with Belial? It is a name which means worthless and wicked, and attributed to Satan. Yes, we most certainly need God's salvation, for the very first commandment of this righteous and glorious God that has been broken, is this. '"*You shall have no other gods before me.*"' *(Exodus 20:3)*

Namaste, a Hindu term that many people who practice yoga use with one another as a greeting, which means 'I bow to you,' is also interpreted and accepted by many to mean that the god in them bows to the god in the other they greet. This polytheistic view of the many false gods of the Hindu faith, coupled with the view that the universe is within us and we are one with the universe has twisted our view of who God is and the rightful view of who we are in comparison to him, our place in his awesome creation, and accountability to him. Will not this Hindu greeting and teaching cause us to believe, if we continue in these views, that there is more than one god, that everything is god, or that we ourselves are gods? How low a view of God do we have, to think that He will bow before another, as one would bow before another person?

What do we do if we have held to these beliefs for so long when confronted with the truth? Should we continue to hold to these false teachings that are offensive to Holy God and in direct opposition to the God breathed Scripture? What rather should we be saying in right agreement with him? Indeed, '...*Let God be true though every one were a liar...*' *(Romans 3:4)*. The false humility found in these beliefs opposed by Scripture are actually man's attempt to elevate themselves to that of God, and one of the devil's tools to keep you from seeking the only way of salvation through Christ.

Indeed, he who is perfect and holy cannot be like us, because of his infinitely pure and righteous nature compared to that of sinful man. Speaking of Jesus, the One who had no beginning, and has no end, the word of God says that he is *'...holy, innocent, unstained, separated from sinners, and exalted above the heavens.'* (Hebrews 7:26)

Is this magnificent God, to whom all will give account, secluded to the height of the heavenly realm to which Christ ascended? God is certainly omnipresent: meaning he is ever present and cannot be contained by human understanding or limits. Holy Scripture tells us, *'The God who made the world and everything in it, being Lord of heaven and earth, does not live in temples made by man, nor is he served by human hands, as though he needed anything, since he himself gives to all mankind life and breath and everything. And he made from one man every nation of mankind to live on all the face of the earth, having determined allotted periods and the boundaries of their dwelling place, that they should seek God, and perhaps feel their way toward him and find him. Yet he is actually not far from each one of us, for "In him we live and move and have our being'...'* (Acts 17:24-28).

But that does not mean that God cannot be in his human creation, who are made in his image? He can and does fill his people who are those that follow Jesus. I am not talking about those who merely proclaim the name, but of those who have repented, having a change of mind, and believed on the risen Lord Jesus. They are filled with the Holy Spirit, who is the deposit and guarantee of the eternal inheritance with Christ in God, with all the sinners made anew as saints, and then unto our eternal home with God forevermore. This does not mean he fills all people, but those that follow him, sealing them and faithfully guiding them through life on earth until they leave their earthly body to be united in spirit to God. Does this mean that those of us who follow Christ and are filled with the Spirit of God, are gods? By no means, for there is only One God, and those whom he saves are his beloved followers and children; though certainly made holy by his Spirit and united to him, whom he is at work in, '...*to will and to work for his good pleasure.*' *(Philippians 2:13)*

Hear the word of the Lord! *'The Lord is high above all nations, and his glory above the heavens! Who is like the Lord our God, who is seated on high, who looks far down on the heavens and the earth?'* *(Psalm 113:4-6)* Of Jesus, the divinely inspired Scripture tells us, '... *in him all the fullness of God was pleased to dwell, and through him to reconcile to himself all things, whether on earth or in heaven, making peace by the blood of his cross.*' *(Colossians 1:19-20)* Will we compare ourselves to this great God? Indeed, '...*"God opposes the proud but gives grace to the humble."'* *(1 Peter 5:5)* If we truly desire to be in alignment with this God, who alone is the Divine, we will seek no longer to be in balance with sun and moon, as people do in yoga, but will seek God by hearing the gospel and turning to him from pagan practice. There is only turning from sin and following Jesus Christ through faith in this life, for after we pass into eternity there is no chance for repentance.

But what did the true Divine do for sinners like us? He, the One God, humbled himself in the person of Jesus. The eternal King of heaven, being fully God became fully man, coming '...*in the likeness of sinful flesh and for sin...*' *(Romans 8:3)*, he showed his great love for sinners. The only person to ever be sinless all his life came in the form of the people he would save who have sinned. He came to save people who worshipped other creatures and false gods, and people who have followed their own views of spirituality and philosophies, in ignorance. He came to save sinners that have had spiritual experiences that were not from God by bringing them near through the cross that they may truly become spiritual.

The Lord Jesus, when he walked this earth, having divine foreknowledge that his hour had come for him to be betrayed, and then to make the ultimate sacrifice for the sinful, after teaching, healing, and performing all kinds of miracles, prayed in unity to the Father. While praying in a place called Gethsemane, contemplating the weight of the sacrifice he would bear at the cross as the wrath of God would be poured out on him in place of sinful people he loved, and to be treated as though he had committed their sins, that justice may be served, sweat great drops of blood, a medical term called hematohidrosis, which occurs with great amounts of pressure and anxiety, in which blood came through his sweat glands.

Our Creator who did that which was unheard of for many, and very rare for some, who trembled for what it would cost him; the eternally perfect, magnificent, and holy God, who became a man to bear the penalty of sin, did something far greater than to sweat big drops of blood merely through his pores. He also shed his blood through wounds inflicted by those who had false views about God. This was no accident, but God's perfect "plan A," to redeem those who do not know him, that they not be justly punished, and doomed to suffer for eternity, bringing them near, by faith in Jesus.

He suffered as he hung there, because of his great love, so that we would not have to suffer eternally. He did so under the weight of the judgment of God for sinners that he faced upon the cross, so all who believe would not have to bear the condemnation of their sins, to suffer eternally in the torment of hell. Blood poured profusely from his hands and feet, as his love poured out to wash away the sins of all who would believe. The power to save people like us that we may truly have life was through his death, and to rise unto eternal life through his resurrection from the dead. He is the One who grants a new life, in this time through faith, and is faithful to be with us all the way into eternity with him in his glorious kingdom, where believers will be with him forever. People who die without him, who reject salvation through Jesus as the only way to the Father, will not be forgiven and most certainly not come back to life again as another creature through reincarnation. Their fate is most certainly sealed.

Cast off the works of darkness, and run into the arms of the faithful Savior, your Creator, the Lord Jesus Christ, through faith, and live. Be reconciled to the awesome loving Redeemer who came to save and make all things new. Hold no longer to the fleeting spiritual life that is hopeless, without Christ, and have life exclusively through the body, shed blood, and name of Jesus, the Blessed Hope. I plead with you to believe on the crucified and risen Savior. '...*He is Lord of all...*' *(Acts 10:36).* For all who have turned from these things, and onto Christ by faith, receive this new greeting. Grace and peace to you, in Jesus name.

17

He Opens Eyes by Love and Grace

'In their case the god of this world has blinded the minds
of the unbelievers, to keep them from seeing the light of the
gospel of the glory of Christ, who is the image of God.'
(2 Corinthians 4:4)
-the word of God

There is a real devil, a fallen created angelic being, who is also known as the god of this world, (notice the small g) producing wickedness and trouble against mankind. Satan is the one who blinds the minds of unbelievers, seeking to keep people ignorant and from knowing the truth about salvation through Jesus Christ. He is the enemy of all humanity, despising us all, and the reason for tremendous wickedness around the world. Because of the deceitfulness of sin sinners are kept blinded from true spiritual understanding, and good news stolen from many by the devil who is also known as the father of all lies, while using people to propagate error and distort truth. Though he be strong among the unbelieving and those without understanding in this age, he is powerless against the holy God of heaven and creation, who holds the power over life and death.

Holy God is righteous and omnipotent, and followers of Jesus will overcome the devil by faith in Christ, giving us authority to tread over all the power of the evil one, our enemy. He opens eyes by love and grace through a change of mind and faith in the sinless sacrifice and resurrection of Christ. He delivers us from the dominion of darkness to his liberating light. He equips us to wrestle against and resist the devil, and have him flee through steadfastness in faith, with his reserved end to be put in hell, the eternal dwelling prepared for Satan and his fallen legions of angels, with all who rejected the good news of forgiveness of sins and salvation though Christ Jesus, because of their hatred of the truth.

Be not ignorant of the devils designs to keep you in ignorant bliss, "heading for hell in a handbasket," as you continue in unbelief, for he seeks to take you with him. Rather, look to the good God who is the giver of life, granting salvation through the good news of the gospel, and delivering souls by faith in his holy Son, unto God's kingdom, and to eternal life with the God we know with a capital G; for he is good and glorious, and greater than all, having joy and peace with him forevermore. May we have life in the name of his Son, Jesus, the One God created us through, for he is the Way, the Truth, and the Life.

18

....

Only One Holy Spirit

There are many spirits in the world, but only One Holy Spirit. The spirits may lead you, and most certainly in error, but only the Holy Spirit would lead you in all truth. The spirits lead to destruction, and the Holy Spirit to eternal life. He is the One that believers are sealed with unto the day of redemption. He intercedes for Christ's followers during prayer, and supernaturally reveals spiritual truths from God's word to us, granting understanding to what Jesus has done and said, and bringing his words to mind. He convicts the world of sin, of righteousness, and of judgment. He produces good spiritual fruit in the children of God, and has power to give new life to all he is sent to. The Holy Spirit also equips God's people for service with a gift of the Spirit so that they may powerfully serve one another.

Have you been born again by the Spirit who is poured into hearts through love, receiving the new life from God through faith in Christ? *'Now the Lord is the Spirit, and where the Spirit of the Lord is, there is freedom.' (2 Corinthians 3:17)* He sets people free from the bondage to sin of all kinds, and also from various kinds of opposing spirituality, which can be found in false religious beliefs and practices. Take no confidence in your own way, but in Christ alone. All other roads lead to death. Change your mind towards

God, and believe in Christ, trusting in his sacrifice for your sins, and you too will receive the Holy Spirit. Jesus said, *"If you then, who are evil, know how to give good gifts to your children, how much more will the heavenly Father give the Holy Spirit to those who ask him!"* (Luke 11:13) Have you received God's gracious gift, not only being born by the flesh, but again by the Spirit?

> '...*"Truly, truly, I say to you, unless one is born again*
> *he cannot see the kingdom of God."'* (John 3:3)
> -Jesus the Faithful and True

19

How Did You Fare Against the Ten Commandments?

"'You shall have no other gods before me.'"
(Exodus 20:3)

"'You shall not make for yourself a carved image, or any
likeness of anything that is in heaven above, or that is in the
earth beneath, or that is in the water under the earth. You
shall not bow down to them or serve them, for I the Lord your
God am a jealous God, visiting the iniquity of the fathers
on the children to the third and the fourth generation of
those who hate me, but showing steadfast love to thousands
of those who love me and keep my commandments.'"
(Exodus 20:4-6)

"'You shall not take the name of the Lord your God in vain, for the
Lord will not hold him guiltless who takes his name in vain.'"
(Exodus 20:7)

"Remember the Sabbath day, to keep it holy. Six days you shall labor, and do all your work, but the seventh day is a Sabbath to the Lord your God..."
(Exodus 20:8-10)

"Honor your father and your mother, that your days may be long in the land that the Lord your God is giving you."
(Exodus 20:12)

"You shall not murder."
(Exodus 20:13)

"You shall not commit adultery."
(Exodus 20:14)

"You shall not steal."
(Exodus 20:15)

"You shall not bear false witness against your neighbor."
(Exodus 20:16)

"You shall not covet,"..."anything that is your neighbor's."
(Exodus 20:17)
-the word of God

How did you fare against the Ten Commandments? The word of God says, *'...whoever keeps the whole law but fails in one point has become accountable for all of it.' (James 2:10)* That means breaking even one commandment of God pronounces you just as guilty as breaking all of the commandments of God. His law demands perfection. God is not like us. He is holy and perfectly righteous and will judge those who sin, for he will not allow sin into heaven. The judgment of someone found in sin is the condemnation of eternal hell, a place of flame and torment. Most definitely, all who are still in their sins are under this condemnation already. There is nothing good you could do to take away your sins, and no good deed good enough to take away the judgment. God shows no partiality by ones "good deeds". The word of God says, '...*all our righteous deeds are like a polluted garment...*' *(Isaiah 64:6)* to God.

God knows our sinful hearts. He knows we cannot save ourselves. Our own consciences witness against us. We are heading to hell with no way to save ourselves from our stains of sin. But God who is holy is also loving, merciful, and gracious. God became a man in the person of Jesus, the Christ. God humbled himself and became a man by miracle, being born of a virgin. He lived life perfectly, without sin. He lived holy all of his life, never breaking the commandments of God. He healed the sick, he cast out demons from the demon possessed, and raised the dead. He also forgave sins. Then he willingly went to the cross and was nailed to it. It was the reason he came. He, known as the Lamb of God, came to be the spotless sacrifice for sin, not having any of sins defiling stains. Jesus took the wrath of God upon himself for sinners, satisfying full payment for our sins. The word of God says, '*For our sake he made him to be sin who knew no sin, so that in him we might become the righteousness of God.*' *(2 Corinthians 5:21)* Then, at the appointed time, he willingly breathed his last and died on that cross. But that was not the end for Jesus, for if it was we would have no hope. After three days he rose from the dead, forever defeating death. He did just as the prophecies about him said he would, for he is God, the Blessed Hope.

The Eternal calls all people everywhere to repent, that we may have a change of mind, turning from sin, which is missing the mark of moral perfection with God, and to believe that Jesus Christ paid for all your sins against God on the cross, and rose from the dead. That is God's holy love for sinners, and the only way to receive forgiveness for the offense of your sins. We need his grace that we may be made right by him. He grants believers eternal life by this grace and protects us from his righteous judgment of hell for our sins.

Look again at those commandments. You need Christ! God does not forgive those that reject his good news of salvation, and there is no hope beyond your last breath in this life. God washes those who believe by the blood of Jesus, having cleansed them from all the defilements of sin, fills them with the Holy Spirit, and clothes them with the righteousness of Christ, making them heaven bound. The proof of this is a transformed life, loving God above all, loving the things he loves, and hating the things he hates, being set free from the sins that we were powerless over, and enslaved to. All things are new, having this new life from God.

May the Lord grant the reader this indescribable, undeserved, free gift. For we deserve judgment, but God provides grace. I failed miserably when face to face with God's commandments, and yet was granted this grace by God, already knowing I'm granted entrance into Heaven, and welcomed and approved by God. So I beg you this day, to be reconciled to God that you too may be forgiven, know this great God, and have eternal life. What a holy, merciful, and awesome God, Father, and friend.

20

Paths, Plans, Pains, Peace and Purpose

*'Many are the plans in the mind of a man, but it
is the purpose of the Lord that will stand.'*
(Proverbs 19:21)

*'For I know the plans I have for you, declares the Lord, plans
for welfare and not for evil, to give you a future and a hope.'*
(Jeremiah 29:11)

*'A man's steps are from the Lord; how then
can man understand his way?'*
(Proverbs 20:24)

*'And we know that for those who love God all things work together
for good, for those who are called according to his purpose.'*
(Romans 8:28)

*'For we are his workmanship, created in Christ Jesus for good works,
which God prepared beforehand, that we should walk in them.'*
(Ephesians 2:10)
-the word of God

Some of the greatest molding to the Christian walk with the Lord Jesus can be the most painful. Some of the greatest lessons are the least liked. Some of the newest steps of faith come when the path you were on comes to an end, with no other option but to rely on God to open a new door as the other closes behind you. It may be difficult, especially when we naturally try planning our tomorrows, but when the changes come abruptly, in complete surprise today.

What is it that tomorrow will bring? Where can I go now, or what shall I do? These are real questions of real life, and no one is immune from them. Some are driven to despair and deep depression. Maybe it is the loss of a job, the death of a loved one, an illness, or some other life changing event. Like a trees branches that sway with a strong wind, our faith may be tested by something unforeseen in our path, shaking the life that has grown comfortable. What do you do when plans fall apart? What do you do in times like these? We have all had them, and if not, they will come.

For those who rely on themselves, it is a hard road and easily discouraging. Hopelessness is very near to the self-reliant, and many bail out of the situation by looking for distractions of many kinds. I was one of them. Wanting to be king of my castle, and ruler of my own path was at best lonely, destructive, and plain vanity. What has changed? How can I dust myself off and begin again when trials, tribulations, and life altering changes come?

God: God is there. Jesus is in my life. I don't have to have all the answers, no matter how much I want to know it all. I don't have to know what tomorrow will bring, for I know who will pick me up when I fall. I know who is sovereign over my life, and everything he allows in is good and has a purpose. He gives and he takes away, and I will trust in all he does, as I should. He guides me, he leads me, and he has a purpose for all that may be seen as difficult. He takes away the old and brings the new. He never stops with his love, for it is unfailing; for all known by him in truth know this certainty. He comforts *'the brokenhearted and saves the crushed in spirit.' (Psalm 34:18)* He knows the thoughts and pains of his children's hearts, and is compassionate. He is never far, and always near to his people who trust in him. He goes with us, and never casts us aside.

The hope in Jesus is a real hope, for God is One of truth, and hears when we who know him call. He will help us stand and show us a new way and new path that he has already had planned beforehand. He is our God and Father, who sees the beginning and the end. He helps us, sends us, and goes with us, and with him there is a friend. So will I wallow on and on with no comfort in sight? I have the greatest Comforter, and his ways are always right. If you do not know this awesome God may you turn from your sin and to him, through faith in the sinless life, sacrificial death, and resurrection of Jesus this day. He will give you forgiveness, understanding, guidance, mercy, and peace along life's bumpy highway.

21

···

False into Faithful Witnesses

Lies: they have destroyed countless marriages and torn families apart. Close friends have become untrusting of the words of the other, and even have turned into enemies, hating one another. Coalitions and treaties between countries have been broken because the parties did not keep their words that sounded convincing, dripping with honey, yet were cloaked with deception. Many have taken the stand and swore to speak the truth, and yet bore false witness against another, discrediting their neighbor. The days of hand-shakes in agreement seem something of the distant past, that if any do agree in this way and stick to their agreement it is found to be strange. The word of God says, '"*You shall not bear false witness against your neighbor.*' (Exodus 20:16)* It also says, '*...you shall not deal falsely; you shall not lie to one another.*' (Leviticus 19:11)*

Many think it is all well and good if we tell partial truths, and as though it is no big deal to tell "little white lies." The word of truth says, '*A faithful witness does not lie, but a false witness breathes out lies.*' (Proverbs 14:5)* The word of righteousness makes it clear that '*...no lie is of the truth.*' (1 John 2:21)* Does that make us a faithful or a false witness?

Many flatter their neighbors, business partners, teachers, acquaintances, and even loved ones. We go about with flatteries pouring forth from our lips, like a spout, and it is done with smiles upon our faces. We speak praise when we flatter another, but it is insincere.

Why do we do these things, and what is the underlying cause? The word of righteousness reveals that it is pride and hatred that is exhibited when we lie to another. *'Whoever hates disguises himself with his lips and harbors deceit in his heart...' (Proverbs 26:24).* Because of what we harbor in our hearts we deceive with our lips, being untruthful and fake. Holy Scripture teaches, we flatter ourselves in our boasting to hide what dwells within us, and we also flatter others, being double tongued and double hearted, to show partiality for favor, and for personal gain. Also, *'A man who flatters his neighbor spreads a net for his feet.' (Proverbs 29:5)* The flatterers deception is also to spring a trap in some way for the one they are flattering. We hear of lying's purpose, and flatteries result in the following: *'A lying tongue hates its victims, and a flattering mouth works ruin.' (Proverbs 26:28)* The mindset for the liar and flatterer are *'..."With our tongue we will prevail, our lips are with us; who is master over us?"' (Psalm 12:4)* The belief is sweet-talking one's way through life, and getting one's way at any cost, no matter who we deceived, and with no fear or accountability for one's personal actions.

Many of us try to justify ourselves in the sin of lying and flattery, even when caught in our deceit. The word of wisdom reveals, *'Like a madman who throws firebrands, arrows, and death is the man who deceives his neighbor and says "I am only joking!"' (Proverbs 26:18-19)* We also deceive ourselves with self-deception, and say that we have not sinned, though the word of God clearly reveals that *'If we say we have no sin, we deceive ourselves, and the truth is not in us.' (1 John 1:8)*

The word of God reveals our guilt. It shows us our true intent, and how we are not right in the sight of God who is holy, to whom we are all accountable. *'...For we will all stand before the judgment seat of God; for it is written, "As I live, says the Lord, every knee shall bow to me, and every tongue shall confess to God." So then each of us will give an account of himself to God.' (Romans 14:10-12)* He is the God who never lies, for *'...it is impossible for God to lie...' (Hebrews 6:18).* With him *'...there is no variation or shadow due to change.' (James 1:17)* No doubt, *'God is a righteous judge, and a God who feels indignation every day.' (Psalm 7:11)* He is the One who loves righteousness, and hates wickedness, and will judge us according to our deeds.

We were made by God, in his image, and have sinned against others made in the image of God as well, and by so doing sinning against our Creator. We knew it was wrong, our consciences bearing witness, and have done it anyways. How do we right the wrongs we have done? How do we redeem ourselves? Many try to "be a better person," yet their sins have not left them. They deceive themselves into thinking they are on the righteous path by modifying their behavior, while trying to hide their sins from themselves, others, and God with their lies. Yet, their sins are still there, and visible to he who sees everything. We say "only God can judge me," and so he will. We have a good God of perfect righteousness, and has righteous anger toward mankind for our wickedness.

This same God, who knows what is in our hearts, that we disguise and contrive deception with, is also the God of love. He knows that we are all guilty, and we cannot save ourselves. We need someone truly righteous to deliver us, who is kind and merciful. We need someone else to pay for what we have done, to take our place, and to change us. But what hope is there in mere men? We need God to do it all. Who will sacrifice himself on our behalf? Who will deliver me from my lying lips, and flattering tongue that has worked ruin, and my false witness against another image bearer of God?

God's love is revealed from heaven, when the eternal Son of God came to earth. Jesus is the One who is *'...full of grace and truth.' (John 1:14)* Indeed, *'...grace and truth came through Jesus Christ.' (John 1:17)* He is the promised Anointed One, being the Christ, to come and save sinners. He came to save liars, flatterers, slanderers, and swindlers: the underhanded of all kinds. Just as our sin brings forth death and judgment, the righteousness of Christ brings life in truth, by grace, which is God's favor that is unmerited. It is given to people that do not deserve it, through faith. He is the One who lived perfectly, for he is the fullness of the eternal God, who became fully man. He did so in love, to save sinners. He lived among people just like us, with natures like our very own. He sat and walked among deceivers and showed love, and spoke truth. He did not accept falsehood, but showed compassion. He did not teach them to do better, to offset their sins, but taught of righteousness as opposed to wickedness, and to repent, to have a change of mind about sin and toward God. He showed them that he has come to deliver, and to pay the price.

Jesus, being One with the Father in heaven, said, *'..."I am the way, and the truth, and the life. No one comes to the Father except through me."' (John 14:6)* It is he who endured the false witness of lies from those who hated him, and the flatteries of those who were hiding their pride, as they tried to spring a trap for him. Yet, he would not be taken away by any of it, but came to fulfill his purpose by bearing witness to the truth. He selflessly made the ultimate sacrifice for sinful people. He came to deliver people like me, a person who has lied through my teeth, and came to save people just like you who have done the same. Do you hear him speaking to you? Do his words find any place in you? Jesus said, *'..."For this purpose*

I was born and for this purpose I have come into the world—to bear witness to the truth. Everyone who is of the truth listens to my voice." (John 18:37)

The word of God foretells his sacrifice, hundreds and thousands of years before, in prophecy, as he proclaimed before being falsely accused and falsely judged by liars full of deceit. He went to the cross, and was nailed to it, the righteous Savior, who loved and never spoke a lie, or flattered anyone. He was brutally beaten, and willingly exposed himself to all of this on his way to the cross, to deliver people from his righteous judgment. He made the sacrifice needed that God's holy wrath for people's sins would be absorbed through the Son, that believers would go free, being saved from the wrath to come.

God's love is shown to us through the blood of Jesus. He is the glorious Savior, who died and rose again in glorified body, and ascended back from where he came, and sat down at the right hand of the Father. He is King of Kings and Lord of Lords, and has the name above all other names. He is the hope of mankind, and every knee shall bow and every tongue confess that Jesus is Lord. This is by far, the greatest news from God that we could ever receive. We should rejoice for Jesus came, went to the cross for sinners, and rose again! His appearing was so important that heaven could not remain silent, but an angel came to herald the good news to shepherds that Jesus was born into our world, at the time of his revealing through his miraculous birth, and moments later, a multitude of holy angels revealed themselves and rejoiced in their Creator who manifested himself to humanity, and then returned from where they came.

On the day of Christ's resurrection from the dead, when his Spirit returned to his body, two of his disciples were met at the empty tomb where Jesus's dead body previously laid, by angels who admonished, and proclaimed, '…*"Why do you seek the living among the dead? He is not here, but has risen."…' (Luke 24:5-6)* These angelic beings could not remain silent, for their King and Creator, Jesus, had come, and returned, to reconcile this fallen world to himself, by his eternal life that came from heaven to earth, who endured physical death, and rose through miraculous bodily resurrection.

He is the One who does what he says, and his words are true words. He is the risen Savior, who showed himself alive after his resurrection from the dead, to over five hundred witnesses at one time, and to his disciples during forty days, proclaiming the kingdom of God. He is the One who defeated death, and sent his followers, as he does today to proclaim this good news to all of creation, until his imminent return.

The word of God clearly teaches, that there will be a resurrection of the just and the unjust. Yes, there will be a bodily resurrection one day, where our spirits will rejoin our bodies that will be raised up from the dead, and we will stand before Jesus. We who have received the gospel, the good news, and turned from our sins to the Savior were born again by the Spirit of God, and know that we will only die once, and will spend eternity with God in paradise: with no more death, pain, or suffering. God grants this wonderful promise of joy and peace with him for eternity, and in glorified body that is perfect, without disease or ability to decay, like that of Jesus. But what does the word of truth say of those who reject the cross, not loving the truth, having no part in their Maker's salvation?

"But as for the cowardly, the faithless, the detestable, as for murderers, the sexually immoral, sorcerers, idolaters, and all liars, their portion will be in the lake that burns with fire and sulfur, which is the second death."' (Revelation 21:8) It also says '…*for those who are self-seeking and do not obey the truth, but obey unrighteousness, there will be wrath and fury.' (Romans 2:8)*

The Lord Jesus said, '...*"Truly, truly, I say to you, unless one is born again he cannot see the kingdom of God."' (John 3:3)* If we are born again, having this second birth that is spiritual, from above, by hearing and believing the good news of the gospel, God comes and dwells within us, by the Holy Spirit; transforming our lives that believe in, love, and delight to obey God. Again, followers of Christ will die but once, but for those who reject the cross, being born but once, having pleasure in unrighteousness, they will die twice, and suffer unendingly in torment, for eternity.

What about you? Where and how will you spend eternity? What do you believe? There is no third option, or opting out. Are you heaven bound or hell bent? Are you born again, or will you suffer the second death? Be forgiven, and be reconciled to God through faith in Jesus Christ. Come to the One who forgives the unbelieving and deceitful through a change of mind and trusting, by faith, in God who justifies the ungodly. He is the One full of grace and truth, who is merciful and is calling you out. He is the holy Savior, and righteous Judge. Who is Jesus to you? My hope and prayer is that our Lord would know you as his faithful and true follower, and that you would know him as your greatest friend. I beg of you to believe on the truth, for Jesus is the truth. Believers have the perfect life of Jesus counted to them, and the Holy Spirit that will produce the transformation for holiness and righteousness, changing the heart and in turn what comes from the mouth, from the inside out. He transforms false into faithful witnesses. He is the One who also said, '...*"whoever hears my word and believes him who sent me has eternal life. He does not come into judgment, but has passed from death to life."' (John 5:24)*

22

The Sword That Pierced Mary, and You Too

'And Simeon blessed them and said to Mary his mother, "Behold, this child is appointed for the fall and rising of many in Israel, and for a sign that is opposed (and a sword will pierce through your own soul also), so that thoughts from many hearts may be revealed."'
(Luke 2:34-35)
-the word of God

After the birth of Jesus, Joseph and Mary brought Jesus to the temple in Jerusalem and were met by Simeon, a righteous and devout man who prophesied about the newborn baby Jesus. He spoke by the power of the Holy Spirit of the rise and fall of many by way of this child, who is the long awaited Savior foretold of in the sacred writings. He has a sign that is opposed, which is the gospel message. It '...*is folly to those who are perishing...' (1 Corinthians 1:18)*. It is the message given through the word of God, known as the sword of the Spirit according to Scripture. It is the very sword that pierced the soul of Mary and pierces ours as well, leaving our intentions bare before God. Indeed, the Holy Bible is clear that, '...*the word of God is living and active, sharper than any two-edged sword, piercing to the* division of soul and of spirit, of joints and of marrow, and discerning the thoughts and intentions of the heart. And no creature is hidden from his sight, but all are naked and exposed to the eyes of him to whom we must give account.' (Hebrews 4:12-13)

We too need the sword of the Spirit, the rich and powerful life giving word of God, to pierce our souls and show us our intentions, exposing and pruning what is unfruitful in our lives for all who believe, and those who are brought to faith. Indeed, the same word that powerfully works by the Holy Spirit to convict and even mold the believer also has the power to condemn those who do not obey the truth. Jesus said, *"'The one who rejects me and does not receive my words has a judge; the word that I have spoken will judge him on the last day.'"* (John 12:48) For some of you who read this, that word that pierced you burns in your soul. Some for rising and setting you free, some for falling because of your hardness of heart, rejecting your Creator and only One who can save you. Know that he does send his word as a sword, but that sword is sent in love, is fruitful, and has the power to transform and give life as a seed planted in good soil for those who receive, and also to damn for the one who would reject it. How has his sword pierced you?

The word of God shows us that Mary was created by God through Jesus, and Jesus was sent by the Father, from heaven to the earth, to be revealed through her womb, being conceived bodily by the Holy Spirit. But Mary needed the sword to pierce her soul also. She needed the '...*gospel, for it is the power of God for salvation to everyone who believes...' (Romans 1:16)*. May we be like Mary, having a heart for Christ, naked in the sight of God and unashamed due to the transformation of the gospel message, converting a sinner into a saint, and a pliable heart that is searched and sanctified through the working of the word in the heart of all who believe. May we receive unmerited favor and forgiveness like she did.

If you have never known Jesus, I plead with you, have a change of mind about your sin, and believe in the death, burial, and resurrection of our Lord, the One who was sent by the Father to save. Believe that Jesus shed his blood on behalf of all your sins against God, and that he died the death you deserve to save you from God's just condemnation and judgment of hell. Trust in God who has sent his sword to expose you and reveal your need of forgiveness, salvation, and newness of life. God loves, and grants all who truly know him to live for all of eternity with him. Receive transformation as you receive your King and Lord Jesus this day.

23

Jesus Paid For the Sins of Mary

Mary is elevated when we are unwilling to believe the inerrant word of God, that Mary had children, by her husband, Joseph, after the virgin birth of Jesus into this world. Scripture teaches that Joseph '...*took his wife, but knew her not until she had given birth to a son.'...*' (*Matthew 1:24-25*) After a dream where an angel of the Lord visited Joseph, he married Mary, but did not consummate the marriage until the miracle birth of Jesus. She then had boys and girls by Joseph, with the boys names recorded in the New Testament. The word of truth reveals what some of the people from their same hometown, who knew of Jesus and his family, were saying regarding him. Though astonished with his teaching, and certainly knowing of his miracles, some said, '...*"Where did this man get this wisdom and these mighty works? Is not this the carpenter's son? Is not his mother called Mary? And are not his brothers James and Joseph and Simon and Judas? And are not all his sisters with us?"*' (*Matthew 13:55-56*)

Prior to the ministry of Jesus, at about 30 years of age, he lived among the people in his hometown, as their meek and loving neighbor, the eldest of his half brothers and sisters, with Joseph, the carpenter and husband of Mary, his mother. He did not teach in the synagogues, or perform miracles prior to the appointed time of his public ministry. They took offense at him, seeing him day after day, without ever considering he was not only their neighbor, but the promised Messiah of the Holy Scriptures: the Savior.

Though Mary was highly favored by God to be used in such a way, and certainly blessed, we dishonor her by making her out to be something she is not, and so dishonor God by elevating, and venerating her. Jesus is the focus of redemption, and there is no other way to reach Father God, and partake of his salvation, apart from saving faith in his Son.

The word of life teaches, '...*he made from one man every nation of mankind to live on all the face of the earth...' (Acts 17:26)*. God created Mary, and like us all, we all go back to, and inherit from Adam. *'Therefore, just as sin came into the world through one man, and death through sin, and so death spread to all men because all sinned' (Romans 5:12)*. Mary was a created human being, made by God, and most definitely had a special purpose, receiving such unmerited favor by God to be a useful and acceptable vessel for the Messiah. But just like the prior followers of God who lived by faith before Jesus came, the Christ would make the sacrifice that provided for that meritless holy favor that was bestowed upon her as well.

Jesus paid for the sins of Mary, and for men and women from every tribe, tongue, and nation; all who repent and believe in the good news, that they can be forgiven, and forsake their sins, by faith in the death, and resurrected Christ, because he shed his righteous blood in place of the unrighteous.

We need to examine ourselves, and see if we are misrepresenting God, knowing we all will be before his Judgment Seat one day, and to see if we are truly in the faith now, because once we physically die it is too late. How will he find you? Is he coming for you? I plead with you, turn away from false teachings and be reconciled to God!

'...But as it is, he has appeared once for all at the end of the ages to put away sin by the sacrifice of himself. And just as it is appointed for man to die once, and after that comes judgment, so Christ, having been offered once to bear the sins of many, will appear a second time, not to deal with sin but to save those who are eagerly waiting for him.'
(Hebrews 9:26-28)

24

Abominable Prayers

What is a sure way to know that God does not hear your prayer? God will not hear your prayers, so as to answer them, when your prayers are made to others to try to get to God. You can be sure that if you pray to anyone other than God you will not be heard, no matter how religious, or how many prayers prayed. Venerating anyone is opposed by God, for God alone is to have all prayers and worship, and so in Jesus name.

God warns us in his word that anyone who prays to the dead is an abomination to God. That means anyone who has passed on, whether Mary or the saints who died and are in heaven. This practice is sin and is an abomination in the sight of our Lord.

By what authority do I say these things? By the authority of the word of God, the sixty-six books given by God in the Holy Bible, that is higher than any tradition or catechism. Many who do not know his word have practiced these things because they believed what the priests taught them, and because many others were doing it, following traditions of men. But what does the word of God say? *'To the teaching and to the testimony! If they will not speak according to this word, it is because they have no dawn.' (Isaiah 8:20)* Many may have done these things because it has been passed down from generation to generation, and even taught by their own families. But what was the benefit? Nothing: nothing at all. God puts this in the same list as witchcraft, and communicating with demons. Hear what the word of God says.

'There shall not be found among you anyone who burns his son or his daughter as an offering, anyone who practices divination or tells fortunes or interprets omens, or a sorcerer or a charmer or a medium or a necromancer or one who inquires of the dead, for whoever does these things is an abomination to the Lord.'...' (Deuteronomy 18:10-12)

God gave this word at a time when people were doing the abominable. In false worship they were offering their children to be burned to please or appease a false god, one perpetuated by the traditions of men. We may hear little to none of making an offering of a child to be burned today, with exception of the occult, but can understand that to be false worship. But what else do we hear of in this command by holy God that continues to speak through the ages, and to us this very day? His command points out that there should not be all of the rest of these things done that we see and hear of in this generation, with the listing ending with one who inquires of the dead, and that whoever does so is an abomination to God. Is this you? Have you done this?

This is certainly evil in the sight of God, and the sad thing is that millions upon millions of religious people are misled into doing what they should not, and so practicing false and abominable worship. Not only that, but when the priests are confronted with the truth, or questioned, they just explain it away and proclaim their authority in their understanding of Scripture, their extra books added to the cannon, their traditions, and their position in their church, as though that would in some way nullify the word of God. But upon careful and prayerful examination of God's word in the Holy Bible, (praying to God alone through saving faith in Jesus), you would find that it says nothing about praying to Mary or the saints anywhere in Holy Scripture. '...*God is not a God of confusion...' (1 Corinthians 14:33)*. This practice is opposed, and that by our Creator.

I spoke to a priest about praying to Mary and the saints, with Holy Bible in hand, for close to an hour, and was surprised to find out how little he understood about Scripture! He may have read it weekly at church, but did not understand what was true, doubting its validity and authority, because he was mixing the word of God with his tradition, the words of man. The living Lord Jesus, responding to the question from false teachers who were the clergy of that day, for not following their traditions, answered them with this question; *"'...why do you break the commandment of God for the sake of your tradition?'" (Matthew 15:3)* The Lord also said, '... *"So for the sake of your tradition you have made void the word of God. You hypocrites! Well did Isaiah prophesy of you, when he said: "This people honors me with their lips, but their heart is far from me; in vain do they worship me, teaching as doctrines the commandments of men."'" (Matthew 15:6-9)*

The apostle Paul, by the power of the Holy Spirit, was used by God to warn us through the sacred writings in Holy Scripture, of people who were, and would masquerade as servants of righteousness, and gives us insight about the devil's distortions, deceptions, and schemes to delude, distract, and blind from the truth. The word of truth says, *'And no wonder, for even Satan disguises himself as an angel of light. So it is no surprise if his servants, also, disguise themselves as servants of righteousness. Their end will correspond to their deeds.' (2 Corinthians 11:14-15)* So we should by no means put our hopes in apparitions of Mary, for they are all false, and delusions sent by Satan himself, who is the ultimate counterfeit. He does not come with pitchfork in hand and protruding horns, but may come speaking religious words, with twisting of Scripture, and a false message of another way of salvation, or another way to pray, even appearing as Mary, and using religious priests: completely devoid of spiritual truth to promote his destructive message. The door is opened when false teachings abound, and are readily accepted, with Scriptures distorted to defend them. They, and the people who teach them, are being misled, and are not following Jesus, for the Holy Spirit will always point to Christ, and his words. Jesus said, *"Heaven and earth will pass away, but my words will not pass away."* *(Luke 21:33)*

My friends, if you have done this, I love you and am here to warn you of this, and tell you that you stand condemned before God for this act. It is surely sin to go against God's command. How many hours have you wasted praying to someone who cannot even hear you, no less intercede for you, or do any other thing for you? God alone is all knowing, and Jesus alone was the only person who lived sinless the entirety of his life. When we do not prayerfully read the word of God for ourselves, by the revelation of the Holy Spirit, we then rely on the direction of humanity with all their frailty.

Again, the word of God says, *'...should not a people inquire of their God? Should they inquire of the dead on behalf of the living?'* *(Isaiah 8:19)*

Sin will be judged, and the judgment is eternal damnation, and there is no purgatory in the word of God either. Jesus spoke of the kingdom of God and of the lake of fire, and that there is no release from these eternal locations. There are many deceptions that men teach and none are the wiser of it because they do not read God's word and examine it themselves, or are being led by people who do not understand it. They drape themselves in garments that have the appearance of holiness, but then they teach opposite from the word of God, and their ungodly actions speak volumes. They teach evil things, as bowing before idols in big church buildings, and show off their traditions, but most are opposed by God through holy and inerrant Scripture, so these priests are leading the people to sin.

My friends, this may seem harsh to you, but I share this with you because of the love of God. The word of righteousness says, *'Faithful are the wounds of a friend; profuse are the kisses of an enemy.' (Proverbs 27:6)* Jesus came to save men and women from their sins, and he is the One Advocate and Mediator in heaven between God and mankind. Anyone who tells you different is lying to you.

The good news is God does love sinners, and has come to save people from false worship and condemnation. He does not want the peoples condemned to destruction, but rather that they turn from their way, and live. Your confession to a priest does not absolve you. No one else can make you right with God other than God himself, through faith in Jesus Christ. Church offerings and attendance does not save you either, and neither does infant baptism.

God *'...commands all people everywhere to repent...' (Acts 17:30).* Believe that Jesus is eternal God who also became fully man, and that he lived the perfect life you could never live, and died the death you deserve. Believe the good news that he took the wrath you deserve for all your false worship and all the rest of your sins upon himself as he bled his righteous blood in your place while he hung from the cross. The One who died and remained dead three days and then rose again is the One who calls you to believe the good news that he has risen so that you too can rise unto eternal life. He is the only way to have salvation and forgiveness of sins.

God can bring you real conversion, not to a religion, but to true saving faith in him! And this can only be received while you have breath, for it is too late for those who die without true saving faith in Christ. And prayers for the salvation of people who have already died cannot benefit them either. The question is, my friend, "is it well with your soul?"

He can grant you what is real, true, pure, and without the lies and deceptions of the devil, or religious men. God grants salvation to all who believe, and those who are brought to faith know that they have eternal life, for they have a new life given to them that they walk in as they live, having a true unending relationship with Jesus! But God does not change, and is not like men. He is holy and cannot lie, and his word is eternal. This life can be for you; he promises it for those who believe in truth! '…*"Believe in the Lord Jesus, and you will be saved…" (Acts 16:31).*

God can change your life from distant to him, and from mere vain religious rituals, traditions, and myths, to true saving faith and relationship with the living God, for you would be saved and sealed with the Holy Spirit, and you would know it, for you would have transformation and would pray as Jesus taught us to pray to the Father. Repent of these things that you have done falsely, turning from all of your sins, and pray directly to God, not in repetitive recitations, but from the heart, as a child of God would speak to his loving Father. Call upon his name in spirit and truth!

God says to us through his holy and perfect word, '…*if you confess with your mouth that Jesus is Lord and believe in your heart that God raised him from the dead, you will be saved. For with the heart one believes and is justified, and with the mouth one confesses and is saved.' (Romans 10:9-10)* May the Lord grant you forgiveness, faith, and peace.

25

To My Dear Catholic Friends

To my dear Catholic friends who are especially on my mind with the recent visit of the Pope to America. You are people that I love, and I know that you are very zealous for God. But religious men, church membership, indulgences, and infant baptism cannot save your soul; nor praying to any created being who has left this earth because they cannot answer your prayer, or even hear from you, to bring intercession for you to God. Faith also does not come by eating, but '...*from hearing, and hearing through the word of Christ.*' *(Romans 10:17)*

Do you know Jesus intimately? Have you read the gospels and hunger to hear God speak through his word daily? Do you rely on other books to try to interpret the word of God, or are you praying directly to God, and relying on the Holy Spirit to grant understanding and wash away preconceived and false notions? Have you come face to face with your sinfulness, tried to be more religious, or tried practicing piety, or attempted, or attempting to keep the commandments, and trying to be a better person to reach him? Is it not like trying to dress yourself up, and put a constant smile on your face to the outside world, while inside you are depressed and broken?

You sought Mary, till you were delirious, or manic. You bowed before all the statues of the dead, and kissed their feet, yet they did not answer, nor bless you. You start to feel as they do, without feeling, and lifeless. Misery is in, and around you, yet you continue to say, "I am happy! I am good!" Yet there is no peace, nor lasting joy, and life seems to spiral out of control.

The "scapulars" you have adorned faithfully, and you have attended the masses, have looked to the Pope with reverence, and sought to do good works to prove your faith. You have gone to the confessional, to try to seek relief, like a band aid, and said all the Hail Marys. Still, there is emptiness, and despair, though you hold to the religiosity, and may even have defended these doctrines zealously that have not brought life.

Dear Catholic friends, you need a resurrection from the dead. You need what is new and alive, and can make you free. Jesus calls all people, from his first call, and through the ages since, to repent and believe the good news of the gospel. Change your mind and believe on him. Turn from all these other things you have trusted in, the outer veil of religious deception, that is keeping you from true salvation, and trust in his sacrifice alone on the cross, in your place, and his resurrection from the dead. Do not trust in your works, or your goodness, by your comparison to others, or your obedience to the teachings of men. Do not trust in their ever changing human traditions. If we were to be judged by our own standards of goodness, then Christ died for no purpose. Jesus said, '...*"No one is good except God alone."' (Luke 18:19)*

Thank God, Jesus did die, and for the wicked, for sinners, just like you and like me. He did not die for people who deserved heaven, for there are no such people. He died for the leprous, the possessed, and prostitutes. He died for murderers, and those who hated, persecuted, and plotted against Christians, like the apostle

Paul did, before he was converted by God. He also died for the sins of Mary, the one he provided his unmerited favor to, that she would be his suitable and chosen vessel, and is himself her Savior. He also died for people who were trapped in dead religion, and sought to fool others, and even their own selves with their pride in their religion, which is sin.

But God does see, and he has set a day to judge the world in his perfect righteousness. The standard is the ten commandments, so it requires perfection. To break one commandment once makes you guilty, as though you have broken the whole of the Law. We all need a Savior, and consuming more of the bread and the cup of the Lord is of no avail. You need someone who has kept the Law, the ten commandments, perfectly. You need that person to live for you, and also die in your place. You need him to sacrifice his life for you, to rise from the dead, and have his perfect goodness given you.

Jesus is the One, who came from heaven, and lived that sinless life. He is the only One to live sinless all of his life. Do not believe human teachings, from imperfect and sinful people dressed in white or in black, teachings from false apparitions of Mary, or from books that are not from the sixty-six books of the Bible for understanding, but believe in the authority of the word of God, for there is no greater authority, for he does not change, and cannot lie. Jesus is the living Savior, and he is the One to give sight to the spiritually blind, and to grant ears to hear from heaven, by his Spirit and the word of life through the gospel. Jesus is he, who was and is fully God, and became fully man, and if you are his you will hear and come to your Savior who lives! God said, *"I will sprinkle clean water on you, and you shall be clean from all your uncleannesses, and from all your idols I will cleanse you. And I will give you a new heart, and a new spirit I will put within you. And I will remove the heart of stone from your flesh and give you a heart of flesh. And I will put my Spirit within you,*

and cause you to walk in my statutes and be careful to obey my rules.'"
(Ezekiel 36:25-27)

God gives the Holy Spirit to his people. He gives us a transformed life, and a heart that beats anew for him, that turns away from meer religion and human tradition, giving life by the Spirit to the spiritually dead. Trust in Jesus who said, *'...'It is written, "You shall worship the Lord your God, and him only shall you serve.""'* *(Luke 4:8)* He is the One who died and rose again, and is the Door to the Father, and our only heavenly Advocate. Change your mind about the things that leave you in bondage, and trust in the ultimate price he paid on the cross, and his resurrection from the dead, by faith, and you will be forgiven, set free, having peace with God, and eternal life. There will be no fear of death or judgment of hell, but only heaven, for there is no other destination that God reveals in Scripture, but a place of paradise, or punishment.

My Catholic friends, believe on the Lord Jesus Christ, and know the true Holy Father, the only One to be known by that name, the Maker of heaven and earth. Know the Redeemer, Jesus, who is One with the Father, and the Holy Spirit, for there is no God but One. Receive and believe in Jesus, for he is the Eternal Life, which is provided by his holy blood poured out for the unholy. Amen

26

....

Do You Bless or Curse the Name?

"'You shall not take the name of the Lord your God in vain, for the
Lord will not hold him guiltless who takes his name in vain.'"
(Exodus 20:7)

"'I tell you, on the day of judgment people will give
account for every careless word they speak...'"
(Matthew 12:36)
-the word of God

The name of God is to be revered, honored, and spoken with
awe. When we are irreverent, and take the name of God in vain,
we blaspheme that which is holy. Jesus is the most beautiful and
powerful name, above all others, and Christ means Anointed. But
why do people use the name Jesus and Christ in place of a vulgar
curse word? Or why do people say, "O God!" as though it were
common? The reason deep inside each and every godless person is
rebellion toward God. You may hear of people from many different
faiths doing this, whether they call themselves "Christian," do not
believe Jesus is God, or deny that there is a God. We do the very
thing that the word of righteousness tells us not to do, and so we

sin. Holy Scripture teaches that when we do not fully abide by the Law of God, and do what it says to do, that we are under a curse. Trying to do better will never do, to wash away our guilt. Each and every person, no matter their belief, has missed the mark, and is held accountable to God.

Jesus came to the people, and taught about sin, judgment, righteousness, forgiveness, and eternal life. He came preaching the good news of salvation, that people may be reconciled to God through him. He then fulfilled the prophecies about him that were in accord with his sacrifice for sin. He shed his blood for sinners, taking the full payment for all who would believe. He had spikes nailed through his hands and feet, and into pieces of a tree made into a cross, then hoisted up alive and hung there after being tortured, and blasphemed by those who hated him. The meek and innocent Christ died on that cross hours later, the death deserved in place of men, women, and children.

How are we set free from this curse? Believers can, without any doubt, say, *'Christ redeemed us from the curse of the law by becoming a curse for us—for it is written, "Cursed is everyone who is hanged on a tree"...' (Galatians 3:13).* He destroyed the power of the curse to destroy sinners by being treated as though he sinned their sins and broke the Law of God, though he was completely sinless, taking God's wrath for sin upon himself, and dying, the power of the curse for breaking the law having no more effect for all who would ever believe, through his death. Jesus paid it all! How can a perfectly good and holy God let sinners go free, and still be righteous and just? Someone good had to take our place, and die instead, and God provided his Anointed One, the Christ.

'For while we were still weak, at the right time Christ died for the ungodly. For one will scarcely die for a righteous

person—though perhaps for a good person one would dare
even to die— but God shows his love for us in that while we
were still sinners, Christ died for us.' (Romans 5:6-8)

His death was no accident, but in accordance to the holy word of truth, the prophetic Scriptures revealing God's perfect plan, written hundreds and thousands of years prior, to redeem people, by faith. A disciple of the Lord, the apostle Peter, speaking of Jesus, said, *"To him all the prophets bear witness that everyone who believes in him receives forgiveness of sins through his name."' (Acts 10:43)*

We are in desperate need of his forgiveness. He is compassionate and merciful, and provided a substitute to take the place of punishment for sinners, his one and only Son. The name that has been taken in vain is the very name, that if we confess him as our Lord, and believe wholeheartedly in his resurrection from the dead, we will be saved.

Before coming to faith in Christ, I was on the highway to hell. I took God's name in vain, blaspheming, and was storing up wrath for myself with my cursing mouth, taking what is the holy name of God, and using it to curse. God's wrath was abiding on me, and his judgment was not asleep. But then I heard the commandments I broke, receiving full conviction, and of the glorious Savior who died for me, and lives. He took away the curse I was under for breaking his Law, and granted the blessing of faith, justifying me by his gift of grace, through the satisfaction made by the blood of Jesus. *'... This was to show God's righteousness, because in his divine forbearance he had passed over former sins. It was to show his righteousness at the present time, so that he might be just and the justifier of the one who has faith in Jesus.' (Romans 3:25-26)*

Come to the One who can grant you repentance and faith in the Savior, the One who shed his blood for sinners, died, and three days later rose again from death. Turn from your sins, and come to the Justifier, and gift giver, having curses removed, and blessings abound. He has the power to save blasphemers from going to the unquenchable fires of hell, transform them, and grant entrance to heaven, and eternal joy and peace with him as they breathe this very day. He is the blessed Savior, and King of Glory. This Righteous Judge, and Creator of all, is also the One who provides salvation as a kiss from heaven. Do you know him? How do you take the name of God upon your lips? How do you use it? Does it flow from your lips as something sacred and sweet, or do you use it to show your disgust and anger? Do you bless or curse the name?

The word of God says, '...*to all who did receive him, who believed in his name, he gave the right to become children of God...*' (*John 1:12*). How about you? Will you receive or reject him? Will you have faith in his name? He is returning again to save those who are eagerly waiting for him, and to judge the world in righteousness. At his very name, '...*every knee should bow, in heaven and on earth and under the earth, and every tongue confess that Jesus Christ is Lord, to the glory of God the Father.*' (*Philippians 2:10-11*) We will confess the truth about Jesus, in one way or another. May it be that we do so as with blessed joy, assurance, and eternal comfort, and not before cursed shame, hopelessness, and everlasting destruction. Jesus '...*is the Christ, who is God over all, blessed forever. Amen.*' (*Romans 9:5*)

27

....

May the Name of Our Lord
be Blessed Forever

'...you then who teach others, do you not teach yourself? While you
preach against stealing, do you steal? You who say that one must
not commit adultery, do you commit adultery? You who abhor
idols, do you rob temples? You who boast in the law dishonor
God by breaking the law. For, as it is written, "The name of
God is blasphemed among the Gentiles because of you."'
(Romans 2:21-24)
-the word of God

When our life and our proclamation in Christ does not match up, we can actually draw the ignorance of evil blasphemy of various unbelieving people towards God by what they see someone calling or portraying themselves as a "Christian" do that is ungodly. This wicked blasphemy should never be drawn due to the continued unrepentant actions and judgments of any true Holy Spirit receiving believer, who proclaims, in agreement with the word of God, what is sinful and what is just, yet doing the exact things preached against, practicing hypocrisy.

God is good, holy, and without error. He is not like a man that he should lie. But God, who is perfect, is saving sinners, and granting them holy transformation through faith in the perfect man, Jesus Christ, who is also the eternally divine Savior of the world; the Son of God. He paid the price, through the sacrifice of himself, to save people from every tribe, tongue, and nation, granting them new and eternal life by the power of the gospel message of God's unmerited favor, through faith, for all who would believe on Jesus' sacrificial death and resurrection from the dead.

This new life is supernaturally received by the believer through receiving the Holy Spirit and the righteousness of Christ, but the believer is still in the "natural" body of his or her flesh before it was indwelt with the Holy Spirit. Before salvation, that flesh all people have which is unalterably carnal in mind, ruled in influence on the whole of life, seeking to fulfill its carnal desires without the Holy Spirit of God to bring forth the holy, godly and new supernatural nature that turns away from sin to live for God.

Now, there is both Spirit and flesh in the believer, but the Spirit has the divine power to have believers live the holy life, by God's grace, as we submit ourselves by faith to Him, that we may not live in sin. When we do not submit, though the flesh has been crucified with Christ, sin may be revealed within us when temptation is acted upon, in unbelief. If we sin, we are exhorted by God's divine word to come boldly to the throne of grace to '...*receive mercy and find grace...*' *(Hebrews 4:16)*, confessing our sins to God, and being cleansed from all unrighteousness.

Jesus, who paid the price for our sins by his very own soul and life's blood, is the same One who is seated on his throne at the Father's right hand and is most definitely interceding for his followers when we fall short. '... *He is faithful and just to forgive us our sins...*' *(1 John 1:9)* but does not want us to remain there. *'For we do not have a high priest who is unable to sympathize with our weaknesses, but one who in every respect has been tempted as we are, yet without sin.' (Hebrews 4:15)* Our great High Priest, Jesus Christ, though hating wickedness, can mercifully deal with us with his kindness, which is meant to lead us to repentance, a change of mind about sin, confessing and turning from it to a walk of faithful and loving devotion to him.

We most certainly need God's grace, that favor that is most definitely received without any merit of ourselves. We may fall short in many ways, so we look to the throne of grace, in humility, for the perfect One who died for sinners is seated upon it. May we not run from him when we fall short, but come to, and seek him, that we do not remain in a way that grieves God and us. God is faithful, and he is loving kind. Our holy Father in heaven loves us as he does his immortal Son, Jesus Christ.

I have fallen short in many ways, but know that God has forgiven me, and wants me to walk by faith, not looking to, or living in the ways of this world that were lived in prior to ever knowing my Lord, but to show compassion to those who have never known Jesus and are currently walking in sin without the converting power and life-giving hope in the sinless Savior. God also wants his people who partake of the same Holy Spirit to deal gently with our brothers or sisters in the faith who have fallen, not indignantly, but lovingly admonish, and gently restore the fellow believer to the Spirit led and obedient walk with God, coming along side to *'bear one another's burdens...' (Galatians 6:2)*, as the word of God reveals, thus fulfilling the law of Christ. The God who is love does not leave any of his children behind, for God is faithful, and neither should his people, showing that the love of Christ we proclaim for one another is genuine. He has not left me behind when I have fallen short, and not leave you who believe behind if you have either, for God cannot deny himself.

May God not be blasphemed because of his people remaining in perpetual sin, for Jesus paid the ultimate price, that the power of sin be brought to nothing, through his death, for we have been set apart, and freed by the power of Christ's cross, by God's unmerited favor through faith, '*...that we should be holy and blameless before him. ...*' *(Ephesians 1:4)* May we believe him that he '*gave us a spirit not of fear but of power and love and self-control*' *(2 Timothy 1:7)* as we trust him with every area of the spiritual and God given life. May God also not be blasphemed by others because of continued false professions of faith, by many who call themselves "Christians," but have never truly known the Lord Jesus Christ. Many are found here, whether sitting on pews within a church building, or on a holiday rarity within its doors, still without salvation, and still in their sins. I was a person who called myself Christian since my youth, but knew nothing of faith in the truth about the Savior, and his power to deliver me from a life of addiction to sin, unto salvation; but at last, through the message of the cross, he saved me, a man condemned, and set me free.

May God receive all glory as we surrender, and submit to him, and his will, denying the self-will, and living lives as obedient followers and servants of our Lord. God so loved us, he sent his eternal Son, to die on the cross for our wretchedness—our incurable sin diseased lives. He gave his One and only Son, to save us from his certain judgment, and our justly deserved eternal condemnation. Jesus laid down his own life, to save the lives of others. '*For our sake he made him to be sin who knew no sin, so that in him we might become the righteousness of God.*' *(2 Corinthians 5:21)* Though not ever committing a single sin, '*He himself bore our sins in his body on the tree, that we might die to sin and live to righteousness. By his wounds you have been healed.*' *(1 Peter 2:24)*

May the name of our Lord, who has risen from the dead, be blessed forever for his awesome sacrifice, by his Spirit filled followers, and also by those who called themselves Christians and are at last turning from their sins to true faith in the Savior, the only way to partake in his gift of salvation, as well as those who once blasphemed the name of our Lord and Savior, having blasphemed God as they also once mocked his people. May we no longer remain in sin, in accordance to the will of our flesh, but rather live such lives that are Holy Spirit led, not wanting any of our life that was without Christ to be continued in, or resurface, but fully yielded to our Master, the Lord Jesus, that God be glorified in and through us.

Do you know him, and his power to transform and eternally save from the wrath to come, unto everlasting life? Do you know the One who can deliver you and set you free, that you may richly receive entrance into heaven, and deliverance from the gates of hell? May whatever is keeping you from him be prayerfully brought before our blessed Lord, who is worthy of all honor, glory, worship, and praise. *'Blessed be the God and Father of our Lord Jesus Christ! ...' (1 Peter 1:3)*

28

....

Are You Ready to Meet Your God?

'...yet you do not know what tomorrow will bring. What is your life?
For you are a mist that appears for a little time and then vanishes.'
(Jam 4:14)

'Man is like a breath; his days are like a passing shadow.'
(Psa 144:4)

Time is short, here in this life. And then what? Many of us live as though tomorrow will never come, or though there is nothing to fear, as in ignorant bliss. Many may even have the mentality, *'..."Let us eat and drink, for tomorrow we die."' (Isaiah 22:13)* Really? Have you believed a lie? Have you taken one of the most important questions there are, as in what is beyond the grave, and came up with something out of your own imagination, to console yourself? Do you really believe all are resting in peace? God is holy, and will not allow one half of one sin into heaven, for he is fully good, and what we think good is, does not even come close, but is infinitely distant. *"There is no peace," says the Lord, "for the wicked."' (Isaiah 48:22)*

Surely we do not know what a day will bring, but he does. Are you ready to meet your God? Do not go another day without a change of mind, and faith that Jesus died for sinners, and defeated death by rising from the dead. Through him is the only righteousness that is acceptable for entrance into heaven, for he is the sinless Savior, who sacrificed himself for the sins of others, that the unrighteous may be clothed in his perfect righteousness. Turn from sin, and believe on the One who died, rose from the dead, and lives on, and knows the way to forgiveness, peace with God, and eternal life, for Jesus is The Way. Jesus spoke of heaven and hell: and both as eternal. Where will you spend eternity? You are only given so little time.

29

....

You Cannot Fashion Him

"'To whom will you liken me and make me equal,
and compare me, that we may be alike?'"
(Isaiah 46:5)
-the word of God

Jesus will never be what you want him to be. You cannot fashion him
to fit your needs or desires. He cannot be made to fit your lifestyle, or
to nod in approval to what is wrong. He will be Savior, God, and the
same as in his word. He is truth, righteousness, and glory personified.
He is holy, and those who follow him will follow in spirit and truth.
He is not a god of carnality and lust, but the God of righteousness
and love. Do you know him who is known as Faithful and True?
Repent, change your mind, and believe that Jesus came down to
earth, lived a perfect and sinless life, and died in your place to pay
for your sins, that you may live. And go and sin no more. If you truly
know him, the One who rose from the dead will change your heart,
and give you a new life. Do you believe this? I pray you would, for
there is no other way to escape judgment, have peace with God, and
be granted eternal life. Call upon his holy name! *For "everyone who*
calls on the name of the Lord will be saved."' (Romans 10:13)

30

....

Please, Please, Be Reconciled to God

Believing in God is not enough to save you if you believe wrongly about him. It is what you believe about him that is essential. Believing what God says by his grace provides forgiveness and eternal life. Do you take him at his living word? The word of truth from the Holy Bible says, '...*faith comes from hearing, and hearing through the word of Christ.' (Romans 10:17)* Believing wrongly about God leaves people in their sins and with eternal punishment to come. Indeed, *'There is a way that seems right to a man, but its end is the way to death.' (Proverbs 14:12)* The word of God says, '...*Even the demons believe—and shudder!' (James 2:19)* And we know that no demon has any hope of redemption.

May we be wise onto salvation through faith in Jesus, the Mighty God, crucified and risen, who through God's love shed his righteous blood for sinners. Indeed, '...*without the shedding of blood there is no forgiveness of sins.' (Hebrews 9:22)* See how great God's love is, to take the punishment that all who believe may be forgiven?

I plead with you to believe in the truth of God. Jesus said he is the Truth. I beg you to believe in the way to God. Jesus said he is the Way. I implore you to believe in life with God. Jesus said he is the Life. He is the One who said, '..."*No one comes to the Father* except through me." *(John 14:6)* He also said, *"It is the Spirit who gives life; the flesh is no help at all. The words that I have spoken to you are spirit and life." (John 6:63)* Please, please, be reconciled to God.

31

....

Reformation or Transformation?

I heard a faithful pastor, Thor Foss, convey something at church that really spoke to me, and was used to lead me to share this message, regarding the difference between reformation and transformation.

Reformation saves no one, only transformation that is brought by God through turning from sin to faith in Jesus. Which one do you have?

To reform a behavior by personal modification is like trying not to curse as much, and to try to appear holy, but without the true faith that delivers from a life of sin. The reformer has the appearance of godliness but denies the power, through trying to earn the favor of the Lord by trying to work at their character with self-help modification. This person is still sinful, and still tallying up their sins against God who is holy, even if they attend church every week and make many prayers and confessions.

The one who has transformation has been shown their sinfulness, turned from their sins to the Savior who shed his blood in their place, believing in this fact, and the resurrection of Christ. This human being is a whole new person with a new nature given them, where they have the Holy Spirit producing good spiritual fruit which is far different from the previously sinful life. The new life now has love, joy, peace, patience, kindness, goodness, faithfulness, gentleness, and self-control brought about by God.

The reformed is still under judgment, trying to offset their sins in some way, and the transformed has forgiveness and is set free from judgment. The reformed is under condemnation, and the transformed is at peace with God. The reformed is facing hell, and the transformed is heaven bound. One may be very religious, and the other has a true spiritual relationship. One is trying to save himself; the other is saved by God. One is trying to impress God. The other is approved by God. One is trying to merit favor, and the other has been given the favor that is unmerited.

The reformer may have a great zeal for God, but not according to the true knowledge about the Lord. The transformed worships God in Spirit and truth. The reformer may think God owes them salvation, and the transformed have been given it as a free undeserved gift.

What hope does the reformer have? There is great hope for a sinner who repents, turning from their works to impress God and all the rest of their sins, to the great God and Savior Jesus Christ, believing in his sinless life, sacrificial death, and resurrection, trusting in him alone, and praying to no other but God, forsaking all the rest.

Jesus said, *"All that the Father gives me will come to me, and whoever comes to me I will never cast out." (John 6:37)* May you come to the Lord Jesus this day, and receive new life in Christ.

32

Wisdom or Foolishness

*'The woman Folly is loud; she is seductive and knows nothing.
She sits at the door of her house; she takes a seat on the highest
places of the town, calling to those who pass by, who are going
straight on their way, "Whoever is simple, let him turn in here!"
And to him who lacks sense she says, "Stolen water is sweet, and
bread eaten in secret is pleasant." But he does not know that the
dead are there, that her guests are in the depths of Sheol.'*
(Proverbs 9:13-18)
-the word of God

Folly is in stark opposition to wisdom. Folly chooses every crooked
path. God's word says *'...the word of the cross is folly to those who
are perishing, but to us who are being saved it is the power of God.'*
(1 Corinthians 1:18) We learn, in the sacred writings, that folly is
considered right and wise to those who refuse God. They consider
what we preach folly yet they do not know that it is the wisdom and
power of God for all who believe. Folly does not want God's ways,
and cannot understand them.

The Son of God on the cross gives us wisdom. It brings us
knowledge of salvation, forgiveness by sacrifice, sanctification

through impartation, justification through death and resurrection, and wisdom through the holy reverent fear of God. The foolish become wise in Christ for salvation and set free from the bonds of sin and death. We rest at peace and with great joy in the Holy Spirit, while we live and breathe, knowing that we have '...*Christ the power of God and the wisdom of God.' (1 Corinthians 1:24)*

How are people made wise who were once foolish? How can this be? It is by God's holy grace and power through the preaching of the cross as he draws people to himself. It is by telling people who we love, the truth, and reality that their sins will be judged. *'For the wisdom of this world is folly with God...' (1 Corinthians 3:19).* Yes, *'There is a way that seems right to a man, but its end is the way to death.' (Proverbs 14:12)* Our sins against the God of perfect righteousness and justice, lead not only to death, but to judgment and damnation for all of eternity. But God prophesied through men that the Messiah, God's Son, would come to live among sinners and live a completely righteous life, meeting God's perfect standard. Jesus also fulfilled the prophecies that he would be pierced through and be made a sacrifice for our sins. *'For our sake he made him to be sin who knew no sin, so that in him we might become the righteousness of God.' (2 Corinthians 5:21)*

For all who would receive the gospel message (good news), that Jesus actually paid for every sin against holy God, we are forgiven all of them, set free from judgment and promised everlasting life. *'...God is love.' (1 John 4:8)* The One who rose from the dead has defeated death. Those who believe on his name have been transformed by God and fear death no longer, for we know we are going to God's kingdom, having the Holy Spirit sent to live within us, in accordance to God's promise, that believers may live out the most holy faith. My dear friends, may we be humbled before God, submitting that we are foolish and lost without him, and see the utmost importance of knowing this awesome Creator. For those of us who know the Lord, let us fervently preach this wonderfully glorious news of the cross, and make disciples, for *'...whoever captures souls is wise.' (Proverbs 11:30)* Let all hear, that they may be delivered from the coming destruction, and live. May we who hear this message know the way of wisdom, and turn away from folly, by God's meritless favor. May the Lord open our eyes and soften our hearts.

33

....

Prophecy of the Cornerstone

Because you have said, "We have made a covenant with death,
and with Sheol we have an agreement, when the overwhelming
whip passes through it will not come to us, for we have made
lies our refuge, and in falsehood we have taken shelter";
therefore thus says the Lord God, "Behold, I am the one who has laid
as a foundation in Zion, a stone, a tested stone, a precious cornerstone,
of a sure foundation: 'Whoever believes will not be in haste.'
And I will make justice the line, and righteousness
the plumb line; and hail will sweep away the refuge
of lies, and waters will overwhelm the shelter."
Then your covenant with death will be annulled, and your
agreement with Sheol will not stand; when the overwhelming
scourge passes through, you will be beaten down by it.
(Isaiah 28:15-18)
-the word of God

This is a prophecy concerning the Messiah, Jesus, and the people
who took comfort in their lies. They trusted that surely they
would never face the judgment of God, or ever experience the
torments of hell. They fortified their false ideologies, and made

houses of their lies to protect them; but those houses had no foundation.

The true, tested, precious, and sure foundation is the Rock of salvation, for all who believe; Christ, the Son of the living God. Upon faith in this Rock, the Lord Jesus will build his church. He is the sinless Savior, and whoever believes in this God of righteousness, who is the standard, Christ's righteousness will be counted to them, and cleansed from all their sins.

But for those who do not believe, the house of lies that you have built will not stand, for your life was not submitted to, and laid on the foundation of Christ, the precious Cornerstone. The shelter and refuge of lies that were trusted in will be overwhelmed, as the soul of those who hate the salvation of God will sink into the depths of hell, in torment, where there will be weeping and gnashing of teeth.

Those who have trusted in God, by turning from their sins and rebellion, and believed on the sacrifice and resurrection of Jesus, have eternal life, and peace with God now, and forevermore. As the word of life says, *'There is therefore now no condemnation for those who are in Christ Jesus.' (Romans 8:1)*

This prophecy is a beautiful one. It humbles, bringing forth joy for the believer, and warns those who scoff against the truth. *'Whoever believes in the Son has eternal life; whoever does not obey the Son shall not see life, but the wrath of God remains on him.' (John 3:36)* Please, come to the Cornerstone, the Lord Jesus Christ, and live.

34

Hear to Reject or Here to Relay

"'The one who hears you hears me, and the one who rejects you
rejects me, and the one who rejects me rejects him who sent me.'"
(Luke 10:16)
-Jesus the Alpha and Omega

Whoever rejects God's message, and his people who share his message, reject both the Father and the Son. If there be no repentance and faith in Jesus, then that person has no access to God, nor forgiveness, no matter how religious and what self-proclamation of faith was made. No love for the people of God and no love for the message of the cross shows no salvation and no protection from judgment. Jesus said it plainly that, *"Whoever is not with me is against me..."* *(Matthew 12:30)*.

But for those who hear the message and receive it shows that the love of Jesus has penetrated and filled their heart, and the love for his people will overflow, showing the commonality in all of the followers of Jesus, that we all have received the Holy Spirit, no matter the denomination. This shows we are brothers and sisters, for we are made part of the family of God by the power of the message of the gospel (good news).

May we who know Jesus not forget to faithfully share what the Lord wants for all people, faithfully relaying his message. All who know the love of God know that *'...faith comes from hearing, and hearing through the word of Christ.' (Romans 10:17)* May it be that the love of Christ that proceeds from our hearts be evident in our verbal professions, *'For I am not ashamed of the gospel, for it is the power of God for salvation to everyone who believes...' (Romans 1:16).*

If anyone reading this does not know where they stand with God, I plead with you to turn from your sins, and trust and believe in God's payment for sin that he made for sinners at the cross through Jesus. God humbled himself by coming to earth, taking the form of a man, being born miraculously by the power of the Holy Spirit through the womb of a virgin. He lived a perfect life and never sinned. He never dishonored his earthly parents, he never took God's name in vain by using it as a curse word. He never looked with lust which God considers adultery, or lied as we have done. He was faithful, though *'...in every respect has been tempted as we are, yet without sin.' (Hebrews 4:15)*

God sent his Son to take the place for sinners, as a sacrifice for sins. Only the One perfect could break the curse of death and judgment of hell for sin. Someone had to pay, and God sent his Son, Jesus, that whoever believes on him, by repentance and faith, would live and not die, being granted a whole new way of life, and granted entrance and welcome into God's eternal kingdom where they will spend eternity with him. Jesus shed his blood on the cross and took the full wrath of God for sins, so that all who believe would not have to face the condemnation of judgment. He died on that torturous cross the death sinners like us deserve, and after three days rose again, forever defeating death. He lives on and will return one day to judge the world in righteousness. There are two walks and only two destinations, so I ask you these two questions. Are you for him or against him? Are you a receiver or rejecter? May today be a new day for all. Call upon, and believe in his name!

35

··

The Holy Love and Hate of God

'There are six things that the Lord hates,
seven that are an abomination to him:
haughty eyes, a lying tongue,
and hands that shed innocent blood,
a heart that devises wicked plans,
feet that make haste to run to evil,
a false witness who breathes out lies,
and one who sows discord among brothers.'
(Proverbs 6:16-19)
-the word of God

Holy God is a God of compassion and mercy, who shows steadfast love and kindness. He is One who sticks closer than a brother in faithfulness, and is with no darkness in him, but pure and holy in every way. He is the One who loves those who love him, and is the faithful lifter of the heads of those who follow Jesus, our Lord, the Savior. He is the God of comfort and all blessings. God showers his children with grace and never leaves or forsakes, like wayward fathers of earth. But, did you know that the God of love also hates? He hates sin, for he is holy. He hates what we do in the body, for we do it against him. Notice the parts of the body that he points out in Scripture. We use our eyes to look down pridefully at others. With our tongue we deceive our neighbor. Our hands are used to hurt others who also were created by God. With our heart's desire we calculate wickedness against another. We use our feet to swiftly run for drama, and with our mouths we produce malice against fellow man, and through all of these we cause divisions with our neighbors. God reveals the parts of the body, because we have used them for sin, which God hates, for he is righteous and good. That is why Jesus said, *"'… if your hand or your foot causes you to sin, cut it off and throw it away. It is better for you to enter life crippled or lame than with two hands or two feet to be thrown into the eternal fire. And if your eye causes you to sin, tear it out and throw it away. It is better for you to enter life with one eye than with two eyes to be thrown into the hell of fire." (Matthew 18:8-9)* Jesus tells us this that we may see our sin as God sees it, sin's destructiveness and incompatibility to life, and so to turn away from it.

What we may think is cute is an abomination to God. What we do and may be indifferent to is what God will judge everyone who has, or will ever live for. Jesus is the One who loved people to death, was buried and rose from the dead, and is returning to judge the world in righteousness. No one is just forgiven, *'for all have sinned and fall short of the glory of God,' (Romans 3:23)* and due to our sinful nature we are at enmity with God. We have made ourselves enemies of God due to our sins, our nature being shown by our actions which we cannot deny.

God is calling all of us to repentance, a change of mind. There are only two roads and two ways, no matter what a religious person told you at church, for God reveals the truth in his word. One road leads to death, an eternal separation from God in the depths of hell, a place of torment for all of eternity. The other road is to everlasting life with God in his glorious kingdom. You are on one of these roads right now. Rejecting God's way through repentance and faith, that Jesus paid it all and rose from the dead, is an acceptance of the unquenchable fires of hell, damnation for your offensive sins against holy God. Are you on the highway to hell? My friends, there is no other way around it, and no other way to God. Jesus is the Light of the World, and is '...*not wishing that any should perish, but that all should reach repentance.' (2 Peter 3:9)* He is the Door to forgiveness, peace with God, and eternal life.

Jesus did not stay on the cross he was nailed to; he rose from the dead and if you believe you can rise too, by his favor, and of nothing good you have ever done, or could do. You can be forgiven all these abominations, all of what God hates, and not face the wrath stored up for all these offenses before your Creator. God is loving and merciful, providing what we don't deserve: grace.

Jesus took the punishment for prideful arrogance, deceitful lies, deceptions, derisions, divisions, and debauchery upon the cross. Being the only person who walked this planet completely without sin, he broke the curse of death for sin by taking sinners sins upon himself, and in so doing he became the curse that separates us from God, that he may destroy it's power over all who believe, through his death, it's power to kill dying with him. He did that so that whoever would believe in the resurrected Christ, through repentance and faith, may not die but receive a new life and nature that pleases God; for he will come and dwell in the believing heart through the Holy Spirit himself, for God is One.

Believe in what Jesus did for the undeserving, like you and me, when he humbled himself and came down, entering into our world through the miracle birth, becoming a man, and lived the sinless life as both holy God and man, keeping all of the commandments, of which we were not able. Trust in his sacrifice, shedding his holy blood in place of men, women, and children. He can make all things new in your life, granting you transformation. He did it for me, and that is why I share it with you. God sends out this good news that the lost may be found, and live by faith! If you believe you can know him today. By faith you can know the One who wants the found to know him as Father, and friend, through faith and forgiveness, so we would no longer fear judgment and death, having no more condemnation from having no relationship because of our sins. You can know Jesus as Savior and Lord.

May God grant you all peace with him this day. Run on the highway to hell no longer, for he loves to save sinners, and wants believers to walk with him, having forgiveness and at peace. Our Lord's name is Jesus. Forgiveness and new life is but a prayer away. Call upon his holy name!

You extend your immeasurable gift of grace
through faith, for all who believe,
Your command to repent is heaven sent, to save a world in need,
Yet you alone change hearts and minds,
and show yourself loving-kind,
That in Christ we shall be set free from sin,
and a new nature we shall find,
In You we fear death no more, nor
anything else against us planned,
But through Jesus we shall know the truth,
and in him we shall stand.

36

Where Have You Been and
What are You Hiding From?

You can change what you look like, but it does not change your heart. You can wear a mask, but it cannot hide the bondage, shame, and pain. Changing your appearance does not hide who you are, where you've been, and what you've done. The gospel reaches for the broken, for the sinful and ashamed. Jesus reaches for those who are sick, diseased, and fearful of death. He reaches for the insecure, lost, the blasphemous, and the hateful. God reaches for those who cannot clean themselves up, and have hidden from their pasts, themselves, and have no hope for the future. *The Lord is near to the brokenhearted and saves the crushed in spirit.' (Psalm 34:18)*

Where have you been and what are you hiding from? What is in the deepest crevices of your broken heart? What is so dark that even you don't want to go there? Jesus knows it full well, for God knows and sees all things. And what does he say?

"Come to me, all who labor and are heavy laden, and I will give you rest. Take my yoke upon you, and learn from me, for I am gentle and lowly in heart, and you will find rest for your souls. For my yoke is easy, and my burden is light."' (Matthew 11:28-30)

It is he who said,

> *"'The Spirit of the Lord is upon me, because he has anointed*
> *me to proclaim good news to the poor. He has sent me to*
> *proclaim liberty to the captives and recovering of sight*
> *to the blind, to set at liberty those who are oppressed, to*
> *proclaim the year of the Lord's favor.'" (Luke 4:18-19)*

You can be favored and set free by God from the most heinous of sins. You can be free because Christ shed his blood for sinners. You do not have to hide behind the facade you portray, to try to save your face. You don't have to hide behind your paycheck, your valuables, your friends, your addictions, your pride, your religiosity. It is the One who died and rose again, the One from everlasting to everlasting, who specializes in setting people free through repentance and faith. Change your mind and believe on him, and you will not have to hide anymore, nor fear humiliation, insecurity, death, or judgment. Jesus said, *"'So if the Son sets you free, you will be free indeed.'" (John 8:36)*

37

Breaking Their Chains of Addiction

'Who has woe? Who has sorrow? Who has strife? Who has complaining? Who has wounds without cause? Who has redness of eyes? Those who tarry long over wine; those who go to try mixed wine. Do not look at wine when it is red, when it sparkles in the cup and goes down smoothly. In the end it bites like a serpent and stings like an adder. Your eyes will see strange things, and your heart utter perverse things. You will be like one who lies down in the midst of the sea, like one who lies on the top of a mast. "They struck me," you will say, "but I was not hurt; they beat me, but I did not feel it. When shall I awake? I must have another drink."'

(Proverbs 23:29-35)

-the word of God

The word of God reaches deep into our hearts and illuminates our darkness, whether it is our secret sin, or our well known ones to others, but blinded to us because it is cloaked in our self-deception. But when the light of God's word shines upon our hard hearts, we receive conviction, if our consciences are not completely seared, and we know we are exposed and without excuse. We hear truth, and if we be people who have drunk in excess to the point of drunkenness, or abused ourselves with drugs, we see that we ourselves have experienced these woes, sorrows, strifes, and complainings. We know we have had the redness of eyes from drunkenness, had hangovers, and have been afflicted by the effects of drunkenness and drug abuse as though bitten by a snake, and have been infected by it's deadly venom. Yet there was no excuse for our drunken and drugged rantings and ravings, our hallucinations, and cursings, for we have poisoned ourselves. It is us who have drunk and drugged, time and time again, and have put ourselves in situations where we are abusing and being abused. We have thrown inhibitions, that were meant to protect us, to the wind, and have drowned ourselves in the sea of drunkenness; doing things we would never have done sober, and wanting so much to have been able to reverse what we have done; it's effects on others, and on us. And yet for many, we are trapped in this vicious cycle, and are tossed by the waves of our addictions.

Many, when we are uncovered, try to hide ourselves again. We try to go deeper into that place where we were, yet the problems get worse. We find that it is not only drunkenness, but any kind of abuse of drug that we use to alter our state, chasing the high, to obtain a similar dazed effect, that crushes us the same way. What is your pleasure? Is it marijuana, cocaine, synthetics, or popping pills? What is it that we take, for the purpose of escaping reality, and to forget, maybe even the wrongdoings of others, or to try to fabricate a joy that we lack?

The word of God teaches us to not be seduced by lusting after the drink, giving ourselves over to its subtle deception of innocent pleasure, and be overtaken by its enticement, that may become a continuous addiction as it takes hold of us, as we inflict pain, oppression, and abuse on ourselves. The word of God gives warning to those who have taken pleasure and pride in these things, saying,

'Woe to those who are heroes at drinking wine, and valiant men in mixing strong drink...' (Isaiah 5: 22).

These addictions not only destroy our lives here on earth, but have eternal consequences, that are staggering. The word of righteousness, speaking of our carnal desires that are opposed to God, says, *'Now the works of the flesh are evident: sexual immorality, impurity, sensuality, idolatry, sorcery, enmity, strife, jealousy, fits of anger, rivalries, dissensions, divisions, envy, drunkenness, orgies, and things like these. I warn you, as I warned you before, that those who do such things will not inherit the kingdom of God.' (Galatians 5:19-21)* This shows us that if we do these things we are cut off from any inheritance in God's kingdom, having no access to eternal life in paradise with him. If we have done these things and not repent, we are reserved a place in the torments of eternal hell.

We need God to deliver us from these addictions and countless sins, which he has done for so many others, as he has also done for me from bondage to drunkenness, and abuse of drugs, and can do for you too.

The big root of the problem for many is idolatry. The idol does not have to be a carved image bowed down to, but anything we have elevated to the place where God should be, and have loved more than him, taking pleasure in the unrighteousness of our sins. God has said by his word, *'Woe to those who call evil good and good evil, who put darkness for light and light for darkness, who put bitter for sweet and sweet for bitter! Woe to those who are wise in their own eyes, and shrewd in their own sight!' (Isaiah 5:20-21)*

We need a transformation from our God, who sends the Holy Spirit through Jesus Christ, the Savior. The word of God says, *'And do not get drunk with wine, for that is debauchery, but be filled with the Spirit...' (Ephesians 5:18).*

134

God breathed, and said, *"'...these men have taken their idols into their hearts, and set the stumbling block of their iniquity before their faces. Should I indeed let myself be consulted by them?'"* (Ezekiel 14:3) The idols: such as statues of Buddha or Mary, that are bowed down to, are not the only ones spoken of here. We take idols into our hearts when we idolize something that we love greatly, or in excess, and elevate in our lives, placing it is such prominence that it becomes what we worship. It could be alcohol, drugs, cigarettes, food, need of attention, pride, pornography, money, false religion; even idolizing living people as children or spouses, and things like these. Anything that is sinful, our iniquity, and yet we put before our faces as a stumbling block, and taking pleasure in is that which will bring our fall and destruction. It cuts us off from holy God, who loves righteousness, and hates wickedness. It causes us to be estranged from God because of our multitude of idols, and keeps us without access to him.

Thank the good Lord, he provides this sobering news, and also that which can set us free and deliver. God himself has the remedy for our idolatrous and wayward ways. He has provided that which breaks the yoke of dependency and addictions. The Lord has provided that which crushes idols, obliterating it's effect in our lives. He has sent the Redeemer to save us from our sins, and his track record is perfect, time and time again. In God's great love, he sent his eternal Son: Jesus. He is the One who delivers drunks, drug addicts, and people in bondage to idols of all kinds. He sets free people who cannot deliver themselves, breaking their chains of addiction from the iniquities they have set before themselves, causing themselves to stumble. He does it by faith in Jesus. He is the Great God who became a man and lived holy all of his life, always doing that which is good and right. He is the *'...one who in every respect has been tempted as we are, yet without sin.'* (Hebrews

4:15) He is the One who delivers us from our demons, heals, and takes us from yokes of destruction, so we can be yoked to him. He rescues us from our weariness and despair, and infuses life, taking away that which is killing us and hell bent on self-destruction. He is majestic, having the authority to grant forgiveness from the evils and sins we have done to ourselves, and mending the damage of sins that others have done to us as well. He covers us with his righteousness to clothe us from our past sin and shame, to have his perfection and life counted on our behalf: making us new. At the same time, he is also gentle and humble, providing us rest. He is the perfect One, and the blessed One.

"'...*Thus says the Lord God: Repent and turn away from your idols, and turn away your faces from all your abominations.*'" *(Ezekiel 14:6)* We can be free from our sins of idolatry, and be forgiven by a change of mind, about sin and toward God. It is he who can fill that place in our hearts, and deliver us. He can transform us from our uncleanness and brokenness: washing us and making us whole. He is the One who has the remedy to all our afflictions. He has the authority to deliver us, through the good news of the gospel message, and grant the favor that no one could ever merit, because of his great and sacrificial love. It is God who redeems, for he is the Deliverer.

Hear what our Lord did in compassion for a person who was afflicted, and had suffered 38 years, recorded for us in the Holy Scripture. *'When Jesus saw him lying there and knew that he had already been there a long time, he said to him, "Do you want to be healed?"'* *(John 5:6)* The Lord Jesus then healed him, and immediately the man was made well.

Let us cry out to him. Let us turn, no longer being separated by the multitude of our idols, and come near to this good God who is gracious and merciful, and sends the Holy Spirit, cleansing us from the inside out. The word of God declares to us, *'For our sake he made him to be sin who knew no sin...' (2 Corinthians 5:21).* It is he who spiritually took the cup of wrath due sinful people of all kinds, and drunk deep while up on the cross as he shed his righteous blood for drunks, drug addicts, idolaters, and sinners of all kinds, though completely innocent, taking the penalty for all who would turn from their way, and believe. He died in place of people he loved, and rose on the third day. He is a friend, transforming the most wretched of sinners, cleansing them by his sacrificial and holy blood, and gives them new lives, making them saints. God's word says, *'Wake up from your drunken stupor, as is right, and do not go on sinning...' (1 Corinthians 15:34).* Let us not harden our hearts, but cry out to the One who can deliver, and has compassion; seeing us wallowing in our mess, and yet says to all who believe, *'..."Live!"' (Ezekiel 16:6)* Hear the word of God say, *'..."Believe in the Lord Jesus, and you will be saved..."' (Acts 16:31).*

38

Merciful Afflictions

*I am the man who has seen affliction under the rod of his wrath; he
has driven and brought me into darkness without any light; surely
against me he turns his hand again and again the whole day long. He
has made my flesh and my skin waste away; he has broken my bones;
he has besieged and enveloped me with bitterness and tribulation;
he has made me dwell in darkness like the dead of long ago.*
(Lamentations 3:1-6)

*He has made my teeth grind on gravel, and made me cower in
ashes; my soul is bereft of peace; I have forgotten what happiness
is; so I say, "My endurance has perished; so has my hope from the
Lord." Remember my affliction and my wanderings, the wormwood
and the gall! My soul continually remembers it and is bowed down
within me. But this I call to mind, and therefore I have hope: The
steadfast love of the Lord never ceases; his mercies never come to an
end; they are new every morning; great is your faithfulness. "The
Lord is my portion," says my soul, "therefore I will hope in him."
The Lord is good to those who wait for him, to the soul who seeks
him. It is good that one should wait quietly for the salvation of
the Lord. It is good for a man that he bear the yoke in his youth.*

Let him sit alone in silence when it is laid on him; let him put his mouth in the dust— there may yet be hope; let him give his cheek to the one who strikes, and let him be filled with insults. For the Lord will not cast off forever, but, though he cause grief, he will have compassion according to the abundance of his steadfast love; for he does not afflict from his heart or grieve the children of men.
(Lamentations 3:16-33)
-the word of God

Our God is a good and merciful God, slow to anger and abounding in steadfast love and faithfulness. He is patient, and kind to everyone, and that kindness is meant to lead us to repentance. So often, many of us hear the call of the gospel, but would have none of his reproof. We hear the good news of God's salvation, to save us from our sins, and we mock, and turn away.

Will God have patience with us forever? Will God be mocked? Will the one who takes God's name in vain be held guiltless before the Almighty? *'Do not be deceived: God is not mocked, for whatever one sows, that will he also reap.' (Galatians 6:7)*

What a mercy it is from God to not let us go down into hell without some sort of affliction, that we may have the fear of the Lord, and turn from our way, and live. As pain let's us know that something is seriously wrong with our body, physical affliction may be God's way, after much patience, of warning us of impending doom. Let us cry out to God for mercy, and not think that he has visited us with trouble apart from his kindness, and will not hear our cries. Just as a loving father on earth would discipline his child who is going astray, will not holy God who is good to all, having mercy on all he has made, correct us, if need be, that we may forsake evil, turn from our way, and to God?

Let us turn from our sins, and believe the glorious good news of the sinless Savior who saves his people from the wrath to come. He is the meek and merciful Prince of Peace. Believe it is he who came to bear our sins in his body, and die in our place, and then rose from the dead in a body glorified. *'And there is salvation in no one else, for there is no other name under heaven given among men by which we must be saved." (Acts 4:12)*

He is the One who is greater than your life, for he is the Way, the Truth, and the Life. He is the Door to forgiveness, heaven, peace, joy, and the life everlasting. Our bodies will not last forever in this life. Pains may come for both believer and unbeliever, but the believers have God to comfort them, and all the way to his eternal Presence where there will no longer be any more pain or suffering, with the sure promise of a glorified body like Jesus, without the presence of corruption, just like his incorruptible body. Turn to the Savior, and rejoice in God, for his great love and forgiveness, receiving all who come to him. He is the gift giver, and grants faith, hope, and steadfast love. God promises to be with us in the midst of our troubles as the holy Helper and see us through life's storms, such as trials and tribulations, leading us in all truth.

39

Eternal Healing

And while he was at Bethany in the house of Simon the
leper, as he was reclining at table, a woman came with
an alabaster flask of ointment of pure nard, very costly,
and she broke the flask and poured it over his head.
(Mark 14:3)
-the word of God

The Jews had strict rules regarding those afflicted with skin disease.
Before there was medical understanding about diseases by mere men
through scientific discoveries, God had revealed to Moses and Aaron,
two brothers, detailed methods of protocol for examination by his
chosen priests regarding people with diseases of the skin, referred to
as leprosy, recorded in the book of Leviticus, written about 1400 years
B. C. (Before Christ) They were instructed in what to look for as they
were to observe the disease on the skin by determining it's effect on
the body, through change of color and depth, with confirmation
regarding disease by correct diagnosis, and it's worsening or healing
found by periodic checks. God also taught them regarding isolation,
separating the afflicted person from others, which we can also
perceive to be for the purpose of the safety of the masses.

The priests were not only to minister to, and for the people in relation to God, but also as those who were responsible to care for the overall well-being of the people. They would determine the progression of healing or disease of the person, whether better or worse: as to the determination of what was considered clean or unclean.

Even if a house was found to have something growing within, it too was to be examined by the priest, and steps provided to remove the disease, even if it meant removing some of the bricks, and scraping the house carefully, with the plaster scraped all around, and transferred to a place deemed unclean outside the city, and then to see if the disease returned to the remaining bricks or plaster; any part of the house. The house was to be condemned for a period when it was considered unclean, or even torn down if it progressed. The person without the disease who would enter it would be considered unclean until morning, something that the Jews, the people there, would have wanted no part of. No one was to enter the house without being considered unclean.

A leprous person was also to be conspicuous: wearing torn clothes, letting the hair of one's head hang loose, and cover the upper lip, and cry aloud, "Unclean, Unclean!" That person was to carry that label for as long as there was progression of the disease, quite possibly for life, live alone, and outside the camp, whereas the peoples dwelt inside, separated from those who were without the disease.

But Jesus did the unthinkable for the Jews, and most certainly the priests of the people. He went into the house of Simon the leper, and reclined at table. A priest from among the people was to come to examine if there was disease in the house within, but not one outside the camp with one who was to live alone, and the leper was to come to the priest if he had an affliction on his skin, to have it determined if it was leprosy. Instead, Jesus comes to Simon the leper, enters his house outside the camp, and even reclines at his table. It was a blessing to the house of Simon, for Jesus, the One known as the Healer, to enter it, but also a time where Jesus was honored, for a bottle of expensive ointment was lavished upon the Lord by a woman, anointing him by pouring it over his head.

What a unique privilege to approach Jesus, and anoint him with this expensive ointment, not knowing that she was preparing Jesus for when he would soon be buried; so much the privilege that the Lord Jesus said she would be remembered for doing so wherever the gospel is proclaimed in the whole world, as we most definitely find her commemorated in Scripture. And what a life changing blessing it was for the person with leprosy, who was considered unclean by the community, to have the Lord Jesus under his roof. While the peoples would have nothing to do with a leper, Jesus did not fear, for he is God. He was doing the miraculous: healing diseases, making the lame well, blind to see, deaf to hear, and the leprous clean. As many as came to him, *'...power came out from him and healed them all.' (Luke 6:19)* Jesus stretched out his hands during his ministry as he walked the earth, touching those who were known to cry, "Unclean! Unclean!" He did not ostracize them, but would bless them, and they would be made well by his healing power.

What about you? Have you been struggling because of the report that you have received about your health, as though you have received the sentence of death? Has the disease or the treatment brought pain and suffering to your body? Are you receiving chemo, or have a disease that many consider contagious, terminal, or only a matter of time? Have the doctors written you off, or even worse, members of your own family?

Many begin at this point to look for a miracle. They start to fear disability or death, and so think of God more, though may only seek his miracle power to restore health, and no more. They seek the divine blessing, but not the greater, which is to truly know Jesus, the risen Savior, and live for him. Though he most surely is our healer, even keeping us alive currently with the very life we now have, how do we respond to him? The healing miracles he provided, even raising the dead, were to authenticate that Jesus was the true Messiah, the Son of God, who has come to be the Savior of the world. Only the Savior, Jesus, could do these things, and also make the ultimate sacrifice upon the cross for sinners, to cleanse us from our sins, and provide forgiveness. No one else could do that for us. No one could lay down his life, and raise it up from the dead. He alone could take the holy wrath we are due upon the cross, for he alone was sinless. That is what is the greatest healing, God taking the sin-riddled unclean, like us, because of our sins, and washing us from them, making us clean. He is the One and only who can take us from the leprous torn-clothed rags of self-righteousness and clothe us with the free gift of the immeasurable riches given by His pure and perfect righteousness.

And how is this received? By faith in the purity of his blood sacrifice through his death and resurrection from the dead. The word of God teaches that, '*...without the shedding of blood there is no forgiveness of sins.*' *(Hebrews 9:22)* And his blood shed from his savagely beaten body while hanging from the cross that he was mercilessly nailed to, was without the imperfections and disease of sin. He alone was blameless. Like a lamb without blemish or spot, so Jesus, known as '*...the Lamb of God...*' *(John 1:29)*, was without the stains and corruptions of sin. Only he could make the once for all sacrifice for sinners, which could cleanse all who would turn from their sins and believe on him. He is the One who rose from the dead on the third day from a stone enclosed tomb, after shedding his pure blood on the cross he was crucified upon, and grants this eternal cleansing miracle to all who believe down to this very day.

Many would focus more on the physical healing, and no doubt it is highly desired, but not all this day are miraculously healed physically. God is not our divine genie, whom we can force to do our wills; but those who come to him by faith in his Son are surely able to ask, believe, and most certainly receive answer to prayer, in accordance to God's holy will, in Jesus name. But what is not *ever* denied? *Each* and *every* person who comes to Jesus though repentance and faith are granted the healing that is eternal: receiving forgiveness of sins, welcome to follow Jesus, refreshment through God's Presence, and richly blessed with the everlasting life. They are transformed, and made spiritually new, receiving the Holy Spirit from Jesus, by faith, no matter if they remain sick, still shunned, or thought less of by those who focus on the affliction or disease, seeing only the outer shell of the person rather than looking into the heart.

Come and be cleansed by his righteous blood, and fear death no more, because of his undying love. Receive the Holy Spirit given as an undeserved gift, be purified by faith in Jesus, set apart for God, and receive the greatest miracle any human being can receive. He is the wonderful gift giver, providing grace that cannot be earned, but freely given, making clean that, which because of sin, is unclean and could never enter God's kingdom, but rather eternal condemnation in hell.

Come to the One who is calling you to him. He is the Healer. He may heal you miraculously during this limited time on earth in your physical body, but do not forsake the far greater spiritual and eternal healing, which is the life everlasting, and resurrection with glorified body that does not decay, that will follow this temporal body. There is coming a time with eternity in God's presence where he will wipe away every tear from the eyes of those who follow him, in a place where there is no more suffering, disease, pain, or death. Come to the One who knows your anguish, and can make your life new. He will encourage, build up, and comfort those who feel helpless, hopeless, and hurting. He will be with you, and never leave you. Even if you are secluded in isolation in a hospital, where everyone around you is wearing mask, gown, and glove, he will not forsake you, but strengthen, and be with you now, no matter how difficult your struggle and tribulation, and lead you all the way into his holy kingdom, to be with him in paradise. Trust in Jesus, the Resurrection and the Life. Hear the Master, Jesus, calling you.

40

Understand This

*'But understand this, that in the last days there will come times
of difficulty. For people will be lovers of self, lovers of money,
proud, arrogant, abusive, disobedient to their parents, ungrateful,
unholy, heartless, unappeasable, slanderous, without self-control,
brutal, not loving good, treacherous, reckless, swollen with
conceit, lovers of pleasure rather than lovers of God, having
the appearance of godliness, but denying its power.'...'*
(2 Timothy 3:1-5)
-the word of God

God is holy, loving, righteous, merciful, and gracious. He is a loving
Father, and forgiveness and favor are found in him, being the best
friend a man, woman, or child could ever have, being our God and
our guide through life. But this God of love does not want humanity
to be ignorant of his will and warnings found in his word, and so
he sends his people with good news and also to warn of the day
of coming judgment, for holy God is a just Judge as well. Jesus is
returning to judge the world in his holy righteousness, and those who
live in sin, and do not turn from their sin and to the Savior to be
forgiven will be judged and condemned to hell. He sends out many

warnings and provides good news, and yet people reject the good news and perish for lack of knowledge. Many think they know better. I beg you all to hear this exhortation, and be reconciled to God.

This passage of God's word is talking to the state of this world and the people in it, and most certainly of this very day. It is a prophecy, and it is unfolding more and more in abundance during this time, and with more to come in these last days with the breakdown of society before the Day of the Lord comes; for the day is coming when God will judge all who now dwell, and all who have ever dwelt upon the earth.

We do not have to think very long to see these difficulties, where hatred, danger, and savagery are so very evident, spanning the globe, sounding the blaring alarm in our ears, if we are listening, that we are in these very prophetic times foretold of in Scripture, known as the last days. Lasting peace would not be increasing, even with all our technological advances and humanistic efforts with regard to peace treaties. We find that the exact opposite are found, with more wars, and rumors of wars, just as Jesus prophesied two thousand years ago, signifying we are in the last days of human history before the imminent return of the Lord Jesus Christ to the earth to be its Judge. Let us look more closely at each of these that the word of God tells us about.

(lovers of self) These will love themselves, so their care in love for others will be less and less, with minimal to others at best.

(lovers of money) People would be lovers of wealth and the procurement of materiel gain, hindering them from looking to their Maker, and real concern for their neighbor.

(proud) They will boast of themselves, high-minded about who they think they are and what they have done or have.

(arrogant) They will have an overinflated view of themselves as they look down on others.

(abusive) These would be denouncing and condemning others by being extremely critical, especially of what is good.

(disobedient to their parents) Children of all ages will have no respect of the authority of their parents as their guardians, and not willing to bend from there rebellious ways.

(ungrateful) There will be discourteous and disrespectful, unpleasant and rude people.

(unholy) They will be wicked and ungodly, devoid of the knowledge of the truth, and so irreverent toward God.

(heartless) They will be lacking in what was once considered natural affection common in mankind, so insensitive, without compassion, and inhumane.

(unappeasable) People will be unwilling to be reconciled, and unsatisfied.

(slanderous) They will accuse people falsely and maliciously for the purpose of defaming another's character.

(without self-control) Many will be excessive and without self-restraint.

(brutal) These people will be fierce, violent, aggressive and relentless: behaving wildly.

(not loving good) They will not love what is good, or those who do it, but have an insatiable desire for evil.

(treacherous) These will be back stabbers, disloyal, unfaithful, and will betray.

(reckless) They will be without regard to their safety, or others, and without much thought of consequence for their actions.

(swollen with conceit) These will be so very puffed up, and blinded with excessive conceit in themselves, being vain and narcissistic.

(lovers of pleasure rather than lovers of God) They will love their own gratification and enjoyment, with addictive intensity, than any possible love for their Creator: being hedonistic.

(having the appearance of godliness, but denying its power.) There are some that may appear very moral or religious, claiming various faiths, including Christianity, for outward appearances, but denying the power of God by either words or deeds that are against God's word in the Holy Scriptures, sharing a different gospel message devoid of the good news. They may seem kind on the outside but deny Jesus outright, taking credit themselves for their 'morality,' as though their view of their own goodness could be as good as God, or claim they know Jesus, yet their hearts and minds are far from him, both turning themselves and others from the gospel truth.

All these were me in many ways before Jesus saved me, and brought me to repentance and faith. It is surely a sign of the times as foretold by God in his word, and I believe we will see more and more of this degradation within our societies before the end of these last days. But just as God changed me, he can and will change every single person that he brings to saving faith in his Son. My prayer is that you would see yourself in this prophecy, as God's word exposes thoughts and intentions of our hearts, seeing the signs of the final times you are in, and your desperate need of Jesus Christ. My prayer is that you would not only see yourself in these as what you are, but by God given faith, see yourself in what you used to be, earnestly hoping for your salvation.

God is a gift giver and a deliverer! Turn from your way and trust in the risen Savior, who was crucified for sinners, just like me, and died in place, because of his great love. Believe that he died for a sinner like you too! He is the One who is the living Lord and Christ, the Creator of all, the Blessed Hope of sinners, and best friend. Cry out to him and he will be your shelter in these difficult times! Be reconciled while there is still time! Do you know him? Those who continue in these sinful states, in rebellion to God, will not be forgiven. With all love I plead with you to be lost no longer, but found by the gracious and seeking Savior.

41

Another jesus

If the Jesus you follow and love is not the same Jesus revealed in the pages of the Holy Bible, your jesus is another jesus. If your jesus is the one taught by tradition, and not the word of God, he cannot save you. How do I know? The word of God warns me of false christs, and false teachings. Jesus Christ himself warned of these false ones that will come, proclaiming his name, just as he warned of false prophets and false teachers. His word is full of warnings about this, another jesus and another gospel, and both being destructive, deceptive, and to enslave.

Satan, our invisible enemy, sends these deceived people to draw you after them, and by so doing, bringing forth eternal damnation to those who believe or follow in what is false, to keep you from seeing and hearing what is true. When false teachings and traditions are raised to the level of, or higher than Holy Scripture, destruction is near at hand. Can a man in a white robe, or white cap deliver your soul from God's righteous judgment, or point you in the right direction, who departs from the word of God? Will we be mesmerized by mortal men, no matter what they wear, with natures like us, who are made of flesh and bone as we, who have days that are numbered, yet cannot raise themselves from death? Only Jesus has done that which is necessary for people to be saved, and he was, unlike us, holy all of his life, for he is the eternal Son of God. He is also the One who became a man. Those who try to say that Jesus was not always God, even for a mere second, or that he did not also become a man, in human flesh, are proclaiming an ungodly false gospel. *'For many deceivers have gone out into the world, those who do not confess the coming of Jesus Christ in the flesh. Such a one is the deceiver and the antichrist.' (2 John 1:7)*

Before Jesus went to the cross, his disciples asked him what would be the sign of his coming and of the end of times. The true Jesus responded, *'"See that no one leads you astray. For many will come in my name, saying, 'I am the Christ,' and they will lead many astray."' (Matthew 24:4-5) '"Then if anyone says to you, 'Look, here is the Christ!' or 'There he is!' do not believe it. For false christs and false prophets will arise and perform great signs and wonders, so as to lead astray, if possible, even the elect. See, I have told you beforehand. So, if they say to you, 'Look, he is in the wilderness,' do not go out. If they say, 'Look, he is in the inner rooms,' do not believe it. For as the lightning comes from the east and shines as far as the west, so will be the coming of the Son of Man."' (Matthew 24:23-27)* He was telling us through prophecy of the future, that the closer to his coming back there would be mass deception, false christs, prophets, signs and wonders. He also taught that no one would have to point out the fact that the true Christ has returned, because all would know. You would not need to be the one tapped on the shoulder by any one telling you they had superior knowledge of the Messiah, of where on earth he can be found, or the exact date of his return, for all the people around the globe would know without a shadow of doubt when he does return, and in an instant. He even warned believers to beware, for false prophets would be doing signs and wonders, to highlight their false ministries, but seeking to lead people away from sound doctrine and truth found through Jesus, the Faithful and True, testified to by the word of righteousness, truth, and life, in the Holy Scriptures.

Our Lord Jesus said, *"'Not everyone who says to me, 'Lord, Lord,' will enter the kingdom of heaven, but the one who does the will of my Father who is in heaven. On that day many will say to me, 'Lord, Lord, did we not prophesy in your name, and cast out demons in your name, and do many mighty works in your name?' And then will I declare to them, 'I never knew you; depart from me, you workers of lawlessness.'"* (Matthew 7:21-23)

It is he who proclaimed, *'...'Repent, for the kingdom of heaven is at hand.'"* (Matthew 4:17) Turn from these deceivers who quote from the word of God in pretense, but depart from his true teachings. Jesus, speaking of false prophets, which gives us insight to false christs, said, *"'Beware of false prophets, who come to you in sheep's clothing but inwardly are ravenous wolves. You will recognize them by their fruits. Are grapes gathered from thornbushes, or figs from thistles? So, every healthy tree bears good fruit, but the diseased tree bears bad fruit. A healthy tree cannot bear bad fruit, nor can a diseased tree bear good fruit. Every tree that does not bear good fruit is cut down and thrown into the fire. Thus you will recognize them by their fruits.'"* (Matthew 7:15-20) Some may look the part outwardly, but eventually the truth about them is revealed, and cannot remain hidden, if we are judging righteously. Let us heed the warnings of Jesus in the Sacred Writings, and see clearly, that we may flee from these deceivers, for there are many sent by the devil to lead people to hell.

What is the difference? Where is the truth? The Savior said, *"'Everyone then who hears these words of mine and does them will be like a wise man who built his house on the rock. And the rain fell, and the floods came, and the winds blew and beat on that house, but it did not fall, because it had been founded on the rock. And everyone who hears these words of mine and does not do them will be like a foolish man who built his house on the sand. And the rain fell, and the floods came, and the winds blew and beat against that house, and it fell, and great was the fall of it."* (Matthew 7:24-27) The true disciples of the Lord Jesus would be reading his word, and follow him by faith. They would turn from their sin, and to the Redeemer who died in their place. They would hear the words of the risen Savior, and do them, in obedience, showing true love for their Master, who is in heaven, seated on his royal throne, at the Father's right hand.

Let us believe in the One who shed his pure blood and died for sinful people who would die without him and be condemned to eternal hell, yet made the only sacrifice acceptable for eternal forgiveness of sins. Let us believe he did it for us, no matter what our past path was in rebellion and deception. Believe that he died, and rose from the dead, imperishable, so that sinners would be saved, and clothed with the only righteousness that is acceptable for heaven, that of the One and only Jesus Christ. It is he who rose with, and will return in glorified body, which cannot decay, or even receive so much as a paper cut. Any claiming to be jesus returning, or god in the flesh, and yet can bleed, no matter if they even miraculously recover, is devil sent. The word of truth is very clear.

If you are trying to get there with anything less, because you bought into another jesus, or by your rejection of the truth about the Christ of God, be sure that you are still in your sins, and have no salvation. Why tell you this? That you would flee the false, and run to the True, whose words are trustworthy and true. He is the only One who can save, and said, *"The thief comes only to steal and kill and destroy. I came that they may have life and have it abundantly."* (John 10:10) Be delivered from the devil, that thief, and his unholy and evil antichrist imitations, and have faith in the glorified and risen Lord Jesus, who will one day come to judge the living and the dead.

42

Do not be Deceived!

*"'Or do you not know that the unrighteous will not inherit the
kingdom of God? Do not be deceived: neither the sexually immoral,
nor idolaters, nor adulterers, nor men who practice homosexuality,
nor thieves, nor the greedy, nor drunkards, nor revilers, nor swindlers
will inherit the kingdom of God. And such were some of you. But
you were washed, you were sanctified, you were justified in the
name of the Lord Jesus Christ and by the Spirit of our God.'"*
(1 Corinthians 6:9-11)
-the word of God

God is holy, and is a God of mercy and love. But God is also the
Judge, who will do so in righteousness, by his holy standard. No one
is just forgiven. Whoever told you this, has done evil to you, and lied
to you. God's word proclaims judgment on all evildoers, and that
judgment for sin is eternal punishment in the unquenchable fires of
hell. If you have but broken one of God's commandments you have
sinned against this holy God and there is nothing "good" you can
do to escape this punishment. God goes into detail, and there is no
loophole, or way we can escape the truth of his word that confounds
us. DO NOT BE DECEIVED!

This is love, to share this with you, and not hate. I love sinners, for we have all sinned, and there are none who have not sinned. I know people who have done all of these things, and I love them. My sharing this with you is not to condemn you, but to share the gospel truth, and to warn of the future, of what's to come for these sins and abominations in the sight of God. We sinned against our Creator, and have all chosen our own way. Many of us have gloried in our shame and sinfulness, refusing to turn and be healed. I tremble in fear for you all, for what is coming, and have been praying for you.

There is hope. There is a narrow way, and only one way that leads to life. But will you listen? Many of you, upon reading this, are angry, and your heart is full of hate. Can you hear? God will not forget, nor will he laugh at our sins. God, who will pour out his holy wrath on those who refuse to listen and die in their sins, also loves to forgive and show his steadfast love and mercy.

God humbled himself and became a man in the person of Jesus, the Christ. Jesus lived a perfect life without sin, keeping all the commandments of God. He proved himself as God by healing the sick, raising the dead, casting out evil spirits, performing miracles, and forgiving sin. He did this for over three years while proclaiming the kingdom of God, and commanding, *"…repent and believe the gospel." (Mark 1:15)* (gospel meaning good news)

The good news is that God, who has proven his foreknowledge and power over human history, has fulfilled the prophecies of the Messiah, through Jesus, and came to take the punishment for sins against God upon himself, that all who believe would be set free from sin, the condemnation of death, and the judgment of hell. God loved the world so much, that Jesus, the One who proclaimed his death, burial, and resurrection before it happened, did just that. Jesus went to the cross to make a living sacrifice for sin. God poured out his holy burning wrath upon his Son, in place of sinners. Jesus took the full punishment, shedding his holy blood after being scourged, beaten, spit upon, and having spikes nailed through his hands and feet and into a wooden Roman cross, being lifted up to hang naked in agony. The One without sin, was dying the death sinners deserve, in love. The One who was completely innocent took the punishment of God for our filthy and repulsive sins. Over seven hundred years before Christ (B.C.) it was prophesied '...*it was the will of the Lord to crush him; he has put him to grief; when his soul makes an offering for guilt...*' *(Isaiah 53:10).*

Jesus then breathed his last and gave up his Spirit, and on the third day, he rose again. He defeated death, hell, and opened the door so that sinners can be forgiven, for all who are brought to repentance and faith. His perfect life is counted to the receiver of this meritless favor. This is the one way, truth, and only life that is able to grant you the escape from eternal punishment and provide everlasting life. The proof of this happening in your life is nothing less than transformation, for those who receive the grace of God will be filled with the Holy Spirit. This new life from God will be unmistakable, revealed by turning from sin to living a righteous life empowered by, and for God, having access to his grace in times of need.

The Scripture above shows God's love for sinners, and great hope for those who turn from their sins, and live their lives for God, who once lived unrighteously against. Notice what it says after the list of those who will not inherit the kingdom of God, with capitalization for emphasis. *'And such WERE some of you. But you were washed, you were sanctified, you were justified in the name of the Lord Jesus Christ and by the Spirit of our God.'* *(1 Corinthians 6:11)* (emphasis added)

"'Come now, let us reason together, says the Lord:
though your sins are like scarlet,
they shall be as white as snow;
though they are red like crimson,
they shall become like wool.'"
(Isaiah 1:18)

May God change your heart this day, and wash you from the darkness of sin to as white as snow. I love you all and want you to know the One who forgave me much, granting me eternal life, and has sent me to share this amazing gospel with you. I will leave you with this Scripture; *"'Whoever believes in the Son has eternal life; whoever does not obey the Son shall not see life, but the wrath of God remains on him.'"* *(John 3:36)*

43

....

God Created Marriage

*'So God created man in his own image, in the image of
God he created him; male and female he created them.'*
(Genesis 1:27)

*'..."Have you not read that he who created them from the beginning
made them male and female, and said, 'Therefore a man shall
leave his father and his mother and hold fast to his wife, and the
two shall become one flesh'? So they are no longer two but one flesh.
What therefore God has joined together, let not man separate.'"*
(Matthew 19:4-6)
-Jesus

The laws of the land may change, but the Lord does not change.
God created marriage, and true marriage will always be between one
man and one woman. The court of "whatever we want in rebellion
to God" will never stand. May we not seek glory from one another
but the glory that comes from God. May we seek the Lord by faith,
with a repentant heart, and to please him in loving obedience. God
is real, and God is pure and holy. The sinless blood of Jesus, the Son
of God, ran red to save sinners. Those who know him, the One who

was and always will be the everlasting God, who became a man to die in place, truly will turn from their sins, and follow Christ in spirit and truth, because the sacrificial Savior rose from the dead to save people facing death and judgment for their sin.

In love for all people, the universal truth is lovingly shared, so that we may turn from our ways that are against God, be forgiven, and live for him. It all comes down to faith. What do you believe? One day we will stand before God. What will be your words before this holy and glorious God who promised forgiveness, new and pure desires through holy transformation, and eternal life? How will you escape the judgment of hell for not coming when he called you, and not repenting when he warned you? Do not follow the crowd any longer, but follow Jesus who is calling you to come and follow him. He is the One who can forgive your sins, and grant you eternal life. May that conviction in your heart and good news you have heard lead you to repentance and faith.

44

....

Where Will You Spend Eternity?

'*...he has put eternity into man's heart...*'
(Ecclesiastes 3:11)
-the word of God

My joy is not that I will live on into eternity, but that I will live on eternally with Jesus. This joy is not found in my soul continuing after my body has expired, but that it will continue on in God's kingdom, and with him forever. The question is, "where will *you* spend eternity?" God has put this eternity into all hearts, and that is why so many fear dying, especially when illness, and when near death experiences arise. We wonder, "what is to await us when we breathe our last?" Something within us is convicted with the thought that this is not the end. Something is to await us on the other side, but the question is, "what?"

The word of God tells us, and it's truths are universal; yet people seem to think that if they do not know, or if they continue in unbelief with their fallacy, that they are free from the truth of God's word, and that God or eternity will continue to be what they imagine.

Eternity in man's heart was placed there by God for good purpose, for it convicts us, and causes us to question our own mortality as we look to the grave. So many would say, "we have never seen anyone come back from the dead, and so we cannot know what is beyond the grave." But God has given us the gospel message and his holy word that is without error. In fact, someone has returned from the dead, the One who came from heaven, to save men and women from hell, which would be a sure eternal and woeful destination of torment for all. He is the same who returned to heaven after being crucified and defeating death by rising from it, who through God's grace has tasted '...*death for everyone.' (Hebrews 2:9)* He is the risen and living Lord Jesus, who grants eternal life with joy and peace for all who believe on him. He takes away the fear of death through this faith, for we have confidence we are his, for his Spirit is given and resides in every child of God. We know we are forgiven and loved sacrificially by our Creator and Savior.

Do you know the One who fashioned you, who knows your every thought, and can save your soul, through faith? Do you know the One who shed his sinless blood and died in place, so souls can be delivered from the judgment of hell, and saved for all eternity? He is the same One who forgives sin, and gives new life to all who follow him. He takes away the wickedness of our lives, and brings the good, through spiritual transformation. He cleanses hearts with this faith in Christ, and delivers to the uttermost. His love brought forth life through his death, and satisfied God's wrath for sins, through Jesus. We who believe can live with new life here on earth, and confidence of his blessings into eternity, because we have faith and live for him, following him in loving obedience because he has granted salvation, as a gift.

Be a receiver and not a rejector of this good news, sent from heaven, for you. Be a follower and have peace for tomorrow through what and whom you believe in today. Be someone who lives this life to the fullest with peace and joy, with awe in your holy Creator. Do not spend another day not knowing where you stand with this great and holy God, when you can know him by turning from your way, and believing on him today.

45

What is Hell Like?

Hell is a place of anguish, torment, and flames of fire. It is in darkness, and all you hear is weeping and wailing. It is the just retribution for sinning against Holy God who is pure and completely righteous. He is light, so it is fitting that those who reject him will be in flames, and in darkness in flames at the same time.

Their anguish will result in gnashing of teeth. The rejectors will one day be raised bodily from the dead on the Day of Judgment, and cast into hell, the lake of fire. They will be there for all of eternity. They will thirst, but their thirst will not be quenched. They will seek even a short reprieve, but will not get it. One minute will feel like an eternity in this unending state of torment and despair, and yet, it does not end.

Though an hour passes, there are still 23 left to the day. No rest, no sleep: no new day to look forward to for those who forsook their Creator. No end in death to rest from the torment. It continues day in and day out. How much will they remember those who spoke to them and pleaded with them. How much they would curse themselves for rejecting the Savior with outstretched arms, who said, *"'Come to me…'" (Matthew 11:28).*

I don't want any of you to go there. All who breathe their last, without repentance and faith in Christ, go. Come to the crucified and risen Savior, who warned more about hell than he spoke of heaven.

Come to God who shed his blood in place of sinners to save us from our offenses against him. Trust in Jesus Christ. The One who said, *"'Come to me, all who labor and are heavy laden, and I will give you rest. Take my yoke upon you, and learn from me, for I am gentle and lowly in heart, and you will find rest for your souls. For my yoke is easy, and my burden is light.'" (Matthew 11:28-30)*

May God change your hearts, and grant you salvation. Being religious and practicing rituals does not save. You need a change of mind and faith in the death and resurrection of the sinless Savior who took the place of sinner's punishment upon the cross. Apart from him there is no access to Heaven, God's kingdom, and there is no third option, but paradise or punishment.

Jesus said, *"'...whoever comes to me I will never cast out.'" (John 6:37)* I plead with all of you, '...*"Save yourselves from this crooked generation.'" (Act 2:40)* Make hast, and cry out to God who receives everyone who comes to him.

46

The Narrow Way

'And someone said to him, "Lord, will those who are saved be few?"
And he said to them, "Strive to enter through the narrow door. For
many, I tell you, will seek to enter and will not be able. When once
the master of the house has risen and shut the door, and you begin
to stand outside and to knock at the door, saying, 'Lord, open to
us,' then he will answer you, 'I do not know where you come from.'
Then you will begin to say, 'We ate and drank in your presence, and
you taught in our streets.' But he will say, 'I tell you, I do not know
where you come from. Depart from me, all you workers of evil!'
(Luke 13:23-27)

'Then I considered all that my hands had done and the toil I had
expended in doing it, and behold, all was vanity and a striving
after wind, and there was nothing to be gained under the sun.'
(Ecclesiastes 2:11)
-the Word of God

You will either strive to enter through the narrow door, or strive
after the wind. Do you know where you are going in this life, and
where you will spend eternity? Do you have assurance through Jesus

Christ? Have you been given the gift of faith, following Christ the risen Lord, and loving him with all your heart? Do not set your heart on your health or wealth, or pleasures of this life. This life is short, but eternity if forever. Do you know the One who shed his blood for sinners, that believers may be saved from the wrath of holy God for sins against him? Do you know the One who loves and sacrificed himself for all who would believe?

Strive for the wind no longer, and cry out to God. Believe in the sacrifice of Christ for your sins because of his great love, and his resurrection from the dead, so you too will rise. Salvation is in no one else. There is one way, the narrow way, and it is the most excellent way. Jesus is The Way, The Truth, and The Life. Know the way through faith. Believe on his name, and so be saved, forgiven, and have eternal life through the Son of God, Jesus the Christ. '... *Behold, now is the favorable time; behold, now is the day of salvation.'* *(2 Corinthians 6:2)*

47

No Other Way

A godly person I really love and respect asked me about unbelievers, whether I believed they had any other way of salvation if they had not ever heard of Jesus. My response was a very quick, "absolutely not," because the word of God is quite clear. I shared the words of Jesus. '..."I am the way, and the truth, and the life. No one comes to the Father except through me."' (John 14:6)

There is certainly exclusivity with God, and God provided the only way to be saved. Contrary to the host of the Oprah Winfrey Show, Oprah, who holds to the new age belief that, "There couldn't possibly be just one way," God reveals in his word, the truth, that salvation is through Jesus the Christ, and through him alone can anyone receive salvation.

What other Scriptures bring light to this question? The word of righteousness says, '...faith comes from hearing, and hearing through the word of Christ.' (Romans 10:17)

Referring to salvation from God's righteous judgment for our sins, the Holy Scripture, speaking of Jesus, says, "And there is salvation in no one else, for there is no other name under heaven given among men by which we must be saved."' (Acts 4:12)

Some may ask, "Well, what if they had no access to the message, because they live apart from modern society, in a remote village, where they may have never heard of the name of Jesus? Well, what does the word of God say about this?"

'How then will they call on him in whom they have not believed? And how are they to believe in him of whom they have never heard? And how are they to hear without someone preaching? And how are they to preach unless they are sent?...'
(Romans 10:14-15).

The above Scripture answers much. You cannot call on the living and loving God that you do not believe in, and certainly can't believe in him if you've never heard of him. Without the gospel being communicated to you, there will be no faith. But if someone is seeking the true and living God with all their heart, they will find him. God will send someone, or have some way of reaching that person with the good news, because God is love.

May we love the people around us with the gospel truth, sharing it faithfully and supporting those missionaries who do travel to remote areas, so that the people who have never heard about Jesus will hear. The gospel is surely the only way to forgiveness, salvation, and eternal fellowship with God. Only the truth about Christ will set us free.

May we look to, and believe in Jesus, turning from our sins and to the living and powerful Son of God, who shed his blood for sinners and then rose bodily from the dead after three days, that we may be saved. He died that we may live. He is the only way, the whole truth, and eternal life.

48

Turn and Live

'Woe to those who call evil good and good evil, who put darkness for light and light for darkness, who put bitter for sweet and sweet for bitter! Woe to those who are wise in their own eyes, and shrewd in their own sight! Woe to those who are heroes at drinking wine, and valiant men in mixing strong drink, who acquit the guilty for a bribe, and deprive the innocent of his right! Therefore, as the tongue of fire devours the stubble, and as dry grass sinks down in the flame, so their root will be as rottenness, and their blossom go up like dust; for they have rejected the law of the Lord of hosts, and have despised the word of the Holy One of Israel.'
(Isaiah 5:20-24)
-the word of God

There are many woes for this generation, those who reject the good news of God: salvation through Jesus Christ. They will be before God at the judgment, and their woes will be manifest. Why perish in your sin? Why be judged as a lawbreaker, when the way of escape and salvation is through repentance and faith in the Lord Jesus? Why not be reconciled to God and have peace rather than enmity, having friendship with God, than him as your foe? Why not change your mind and be forgiven, having your burdens lifted from your shoulders: at freedom, by faith, and with all joy?

Jesus is the payment for sin. He is the One who sends and fills the hearts of believers with the Holy Spirit. He is the crucified and resurrected Savior, who always was, is, and will come again. His word says, *"'Have I any pleasure in the death of the wicked," declares the Lord GOD, "and not rather that he should turn from his way and live?"' (Ezekiel 18:23)*

God provided the way through Jesus Christ his Son. God the Father who created all creation through Christ, sent his Son to be miraculously conceived by the Holy Spirit within a virgin. The eternal Son of God lived life as a man perfectly under the Law of God. He did it to save all who are judged guilty due to their sin by breaking the Law, who turn to him by faith, that they may not face judgment. *'...He died for all...' (2 Corinthians 5:15)* upon the cross, after becoming the curse of sin as a sacrifice of payment for guilt before God, satisfying God's holy wrath for sin, and destroying it's power to condemn all who believe through his death. He who was raised from the dead, by the glory of the Father, is the One who says, *'..."Follow me..."' (Matthew 8:22).* He is the One who knows the way, and apart from him there is no hope or salvation. Do you know him? Turn and live.

All who do not believe will face woes in this life, and most certainly throughout eternity. The woe of fiery hell does not end, but eternal life for the children of God, at joy and peace, does not end either. I beg you to *'...be reconciled to God.' (2 Corinthians 5:20)* I pray you would not reject such a great salvation. Turn from your woeful way, and run to God who made the ultimate sacrifice for sinners, who saved even an unworthy man such as me. Trust in him and live forever, even after your spirit departs from your mortal body in physical death. Do you know him? I pray you would!

49

Favor, Faith, and Forgiveness

"'Blessed are those whose lawless deeds are
forgiven, and whose sins are covered;
blessed is the man against whom the Lord will not count his sin.'"
(Romans 4:7-8)
-the word of God

This was going back a few years ago, after walking with God for two years in the most holy faith. I was tired from not sleeping well, and from a day of nursing clinical preparation in the hospital, with a headache on top of it all. I just wanted to get home and to bed, to sleep for a while before getting up to prepare for the next day's patient to treat and care for. Less than a minute from my home a police officer standing on the right side of the road waved me over. I wasn't sure what I had done wrong, but pulled over to comply. Leaning by the passenger window he said the words, "License, registration, and proof of insurance."

He informed me I was driving without my seat belt. I gave him my license, and then rummaged through the glove compartment for my registration and insurance card. When he was informed that my registration could not be found, he whispered, as though to himself, but loud enough for me to hear, "ticket in the mail." After continuing to rummage through the glove box something fell out, and onto the door jam, between the door and the right passenger seat, where it caught his eye.

"Is that the Daily Bread?" the officer asked. At first I did not know what he was talking about because I did not see what fell. It was a Christian devotional of the Scriptures they provided at church where there was Scripture and a message within to minister to the reader. He then asked me where I went to church, and that he used to get that same devotional too. He then said something like this after handing me back my license, "You're all set brother!" He let me go! As I was contemplating the mounting infractions of a ticket or tickets for not having on a seat belt, not having my registration on me, and wondering if my car would be towed, was pleasantly surprised that I was let go completely free of any penalty! Praise the Lord! It was certainly my delight that I would not be penalized at all, and would be allowed to go about my day.

After pulling off to go home the prayer went up. "God, what would you have me understand from all of this?" And then the answer came. The police officer was the law, but he showed me grace.

We hear in the book of Romans, echoed by God, what he had King David write in Psalm 32.

"'Blessed are those whose lawless deeds are
forgiven, and whose sins are covered;
blessed is the man against whom the Lord will not count his sin.'"
(Romans 4:7-8)

How wonderful it is to know that we who believe, like King David, though guilty of lawless deeds, that our sins are covered by the blood of Jesus, and the Lord is not counting to us our sins, through him. It was not because we were less sinful than others, or by anything of righteousness that we have done, but because of God granted favor, to give faith, that we may get forgiveness. It was not that we were wiser than others, in and of our own right, but because of God who provides grace, and has covered our many offenses, causing us to be blessed.

Blessed indeed, *"...are those whose lawless deeds are forgiven, and whose sins are covered; blessed is the man against whom the Lord will not count his sin." (Romans 4:7-8)*

The Righteous Judge grants favor to those who do not deserve it, who have no way to merit it, and pours upon, and into us, a holy transformation. May we not look down upon those who do not believe, or have yet to believe, but continue to faithfully share the gospel of God, and pray for their salvation. I was not brought to faith until a few days before my 35th birthday. But by God's grace he saved me then, and a new life was granted me through the power of the gospel. May we not count out those in the bondage of the most grievous to us of sins, but continue to faithfully lift them up in prayer before the Lord. Let us not forget the gift of God to believe, provided by grace.

I love what Jesus proclaimed. *"The Spirit of the Lord is upon me, because he has anointed me to proclaim good news to the poor. He has sent me to proclaim liberty to the captives and recovering of sight to the blind, to set at liberty those who are oppressed, to proclaim the year of the Lord's favor."* *(Luke 4:18-19)* We who believe were the poor, the captives, the blind, and the oppressed, who have received good news, the liberty proclaimed to us, spiritual sight, and liberating freedom in Christ; all by his abundant grace.

For those who know Jesus, may we give him the glory, for this undeserved and unmerited favor from God. May we bless his name without ceasing, who continually blesses us, and may we faithfully proclaim the gospel of God, that Jesus died and rose again, that those who believe can live. May those who hunger for God, and hear him calling through Jesus, receive this faith extended by grace, and so be saved. Hallelujah! Amen

50

The Cross and the Empty Tomb

'But on the first day of the week, at early dawn, they went to the tomb, taking the spices they had prepared. And they found the stone rolled away from the tomb, but when they went in they did not find the body of the Lord Jesus. While they were perplexed about this, behold, two men stood by them in dazzling apparel. And as they were frightened and bowed their faces to the ground, the men said to them, "Why do you seek the living among the dead? He is not here, but has risen. Remember how he told you, while he was still in Galilee, that the Son of Man must be delivered into the hands of sinful men and be crucified and on the third day rise." And they remembered his words, and returning from the tomb they told all these things to the eleven and to all the rest. Now it was Mary Magdalene and Joanna and Mary the mother of James and the other women with them who told these things to the apostles, but these words seemed to them an idle tale, and they did not believe them. But Peter rose and ran to the tomb; stooping and looking in, he saw the linen cloths by themselves; and he went home marveling at what had happened.'

(Luke 24:1-12)

-the word of God

Falsely accused, beaten, mocked, and treated with contempt, Jesus Christ was tortured and nailed to the cross through his hands and feet. He was lifted up from the earth and hung there as his blood poured from his scourged and pierced body.

Certainly a horrific site to his disciples, seeing their Lord and Teacher in excruciating pain as he gasped for breath. This is the One who taught about the kingdom of God. This is the One who taught about sin and righteousness. This is their same Lord who proclaimed forgiveness of sin through repentance and faith: faith in him. The Healer, the One who gave sight to the blind, granted hearing to the deaf, and restored the sick, gasped for breath while stretched out on a blistering Roman cross. The Son of God who loved sinners and rebuked religious hypocrites was mocked with these words; '..."*You who would destroy the temple and rebuild it in three days, save yourself! If you are the Son of God, come down from the cross.*"' *(Matthew 27:40)* Two criminals, in their final hours of life, also mocked him while they hung, crucified for their crimes on crosses next to the completely innocent Christ, saying, "*He trusts in God; let God deliver him now, if he desires him. For he said, 'I am the Son of God.'*" *(Matthew 27:43)* Soon after, Jesus said, '..."*Father, into your hands I commit my spirit!" And having said this he breathed his last.*' *(Luke 23:46)*

On the third day the ladies were heading to the stone enclosed tomb where the body of the Lord Jesus was laid, to anoint it. The grieving women were surely still in disbelief due to the horror of their Master's death. In the gospel according to Mark it was recorded, '... *they were saying to one another, "Who will roll away the stone for us from the entrance of the tomb?"*' *(Mark 16:3)* This same Jesus who had others roll away a stone to raise a man named Lazarus from death had his lifeless body laid dead within a stone covered tomb; the irony! What they surprisingly discovered was the stone already rolled away from the tomb when they came near; but the body of the Lord Jesus was not to be found upon entering the tomb. They were perplexed. First the crucifixion, the loss of their beloved Master, and now this: an empty tomb. As they wondered, they found they were not alone; two angels were with them, dressed in clothing that shined and reflected brilliantly, like nothing from this world.

The ladies were then asked, *'…"Why do you seek the living among the dead? He is not here, but has risen."…' (Luke 24:5-6)* Imagine receiving this report from these two angelic beings about Jesus, that he is alive, raised from the dead. Of all the very many miracles that Jesus had performed, this was, by far, the greatest of them all. He raised himself from the grave, victorious over the power of death. Again, in the gospel, regarding his death and resurrection, we hear Jesus say this to his disciples before he went to the cross. *"For this reason the Father loves me, because I lay down my life that I may take it up again. No one takes it from me, but I lay it down of my own accord. I have authority to lay it down, and I have authority to take it up again. This charge I have received from my Father." (John 10:17-18)*

The angels give us a wonderful reminder of prophecy. They reminded the women of Jesus who prophesied his death, burial, and resurrection. This was something Jesus had done numerous times before his crucifixion. What did the many mockers say while Jesus was dying on the cross? They did not understand when Jesus said, *'…"Destroy this temple, and in three days I will raise it up," (John 2:19)* that Jesus was speaking of the temple of his body, the death and resurrection of it. Our Lord also said, in the gospel of Matthew, *'…"The Son of Man is about to be delivered into the hands of men, and they will kill him, and he will be raised on the third day." (Matthew 17:22-23)*

What many of us may not know is that the coming of Jesus, the Messiah, was prophesied in numerous places in the Old Testament, hundreds, and thousands of years before his coming from heaven to earth, to die for men and women's sins, and be raised again. God shows us through fulfilled prophecy that his fingerprint is on the Scriptures by his omnipotent providence and foreknowledge. God has been fulfilling prophecies in his word from times before the long awaited first coming of Jesus. With regard to the crucifixion, Psalm 22, written over 900 years B.C., prophesies how the Christ would be crucified. It prophetically states, '...*they have pierced my hands and feet...*' *(Psalm 22:16),* speaking of the crucifixion beforehand, as though it had already taken place. And again in the book of the prophet Zechariah, written around 500 years B.C., when speaking of people who would believe in the resurrected Christ, it says, '... *when they look on me, on him whom they have pierced...' (Zechariah 12:10).* These were prophecies from the past, spoken by men who were called and empowered by God to be prophets, saying exactly what the Almighty would have them. Also in the book of the prophet Isaiah, written over 700 years B.C., it says, '...*he was pierced for our transgressions; he was crushed for our iniquities; upon him was the chastisement that brought us peace, and with his wounds we are healed. All we like sheep have gone astray; we have turned—every one—to his own way; and the Lord has laid on him the iniquity of us all.' (Isaiah 53:5-6)* Another time, speaking of Jesus Christ and him being pierced we hear a future prophecy in the book of Revelation of his imminent return to judge the world in righteousness, the date of that known only by the Father. *'Behold, he is coming with the clouds, and every eye will see him, even those who pierced him, and all tribes of the earth will wail on account of him. Even so. Amen.'" (Revelation 1:7)*

There were numerous prophecies of Jesus, pertaining in some way to his life, death, and resurrection, fulfilled with all accuracy with his first coming. There are far more to be fulfilled with his second coming. The One who came and lived a life of meekness and humility is coming to reign as King of Kings, and Lord of Lords. God reveals he has power over, not only past fulfilled events, but also the future.

'*...God shows his love for us in that while we were still sinners, Christ died for us.*' *(Romans 5:8)* We have all sinned against God and we all deserve the death that Jesus endured on the cross. We all deserve to be eternally separated from the Father. It is for sinners that Jesus died. He did it so that all who believe would be reconciled to God! '*For the wages of sin is death, but the free gift of God is eternal life in Christ Jesus our Lord.*' *(Romans 6:23)* The Son of God is coming back for his followers, to receive them onto himself, in all glory and with great joy. Will you be one of them found among the faithful?

'*And just as it is appointed for man to die once, and after that comes judgment, so Christ, having been offered once to bear the sins of many, will appear a second time, not to deal with sin but to save those who are eagerly waiting for him.*' *(Hebrews 9:27-28)* Is that you? Are you eagerly awaiting his return? Does the cross and the empty tomb make you want to jump for joy? Do you know the One who sacrificially loves, shed his blood, and rose from the dead to reconcile you back to himself? Are you fearful of, or through Christ have no fear of death? The call now and in the past, from the Old and through the New Testament throughout the many generations is the same: "Repent." Have you been saving your life for yourself, a life separate from the holy God who made you, or have you received the free gift of salvation because of his great love and grace? When he comes will you be treated as friend of foe? Do you know where you would spend eternity if you were to be before him today, or are you unsure? Do you have everlasting life or will you spend an eternity in hell? God has the power over life and death.

The same Jesus who forgives sin and defeated death is also coming to judge the peoples of the earth. The question is, "who is Jesus Christ to you?" Will you be accepted or will he say *"'I never knew you"'...'* *(Matthew 7:23)*? May we not continue in doubt but believe when God extends us such great news of his glorious salvation, showing our *"'...works have been carried out in God.'"* *(John 3:21)*

We have graves of many whose remains are still here. God gives us a cross and an empty tomb and calls us to come! God does not want any of us to perish but to have all who believe to share in a resurrection like this.

God loved the world so much he gave what is most precious to him, his only Son, in place of sinners like us. He did not do it that we would believe in a really good dead man, but in the risen Savior and Lord who is the One who loved to the point of shedding his own blood, absorbing the punishment and dying, that by faith in his sacrificial death and resurrection we may have life. This is the true meaning of what many believers remember every day, the resurrection of our Lord and Savior who defeated death after shedding his blood for the sins of many. The question is, "What do you believe?" Receive the words of Jesus; *'..."I am the resurrection and the life. Whoever believes in me, though he die, yet shall he live, and everyone who lives and believes in me shall never die. Do you believe this?"'* *(John 11:25-26)*

51

Short Personal Testimony

40 years ago, in the month of October, God granted me my first breath. He gave me a father and a mother, and later a sister and brother. He granted me the places where I would live, and the numbers of years I would have. He showed me mercy the times I was sick, and delivered me from so many near death experiences. Though there was a time where I didn't think I would ever see the age of 21, due to my wild and sinful living, God knew I would live.

The life once lived was in rebellion to my parents, and surely gave them grief. I was a horrible example to my younger brother and sister. Drinking till drunkenness was a regular occurrence in my teenage years, since high school, and continued on into my 20's and 30's, with a few car accidents due to my drunkenness. Drugs, wrathful anger, fighting, womanizing, cursing, and gambling were a big part of my life. So was pride. I did what was right in my own sight, was self-absorbed, and thought of myself as pretty righteous, though God viewed me as what I really was, dead in my trespasses and sins, and living like the devil. But God, in his great compassion showed me mercy, and did not give me my last breath years before, that I would die in my sins, and receive eternal justice in hell. He had different plans. 6 years ago, a few days before my 35th birthday, at a point in life after much tribulation where I felt I was going to die, God did something absolutely amazing. After reading from the gospel in the Holy Bible, God gave me a new life.

He showed me my sins prior to reading the gospel, in the book of Exodus, chapter 20, where it says,

"'You shall have no other gods before me.'"
(Exodus 20:3)

"'You shall not make for yourself a carved image, or any likeness of anything that is in heaven above, or that is in the earth beneath, or that is in the water under the earth. You shall not bow down to them or serve them, for I the Lord your God am a jealous God, visiting the iniquity of the fathers on the children to the third and the fourth generation of those who hate me, but showing steadfast love to thousands of those who love me and keep my commandments.'"
(Exodus 20:4-6)

"'You shall not take the name of the Lord your God in vain, for the Lord will not hold him guiltless who takes his name in vain.'"
(Exodus 20:7)

"'Remember the Sabbath day, to keep it holy. Six days you shall labor, and do all your work, but the seventh day is a Sabbath to the Lord your God.'"
(Exodus 20:8-10)

"'Honor your father and your mother, that your days may be long in the land that the Lord your God is giving you.'"
(Exodus 20:12)

"'You shall not murder.'"
(Exodus 20:13)

"'You shall not commit adultery.'"
(Exodus 20:14)

"'You shall not steal.'"
(Exodus 20:15)

"'You shall not bear false witness against your neighbor.'"
(Exodus 20:16)

"'You shall not covet"..."anything that is your neighbor's.'"
(Exodus 20:17)

After reading these, he showed me how far away I was from his perfection, and glory. The word of God says, '...*be sure your sin will find you out.*' (Numbers 32:23) And so it did. And then finally, I read of the divine Savior, Jesus, who came from heaven to earth by the Holy Spirit. Though the eternal God, he became fully man as well. He lived a perfect life, keeping all the commandments. Though Creator of all things, he came to serve his creation made in his image, men and women, to save us from our sins. Though completely righteous, he broke bread with sinners, and stretched out his hands to heal the diseased, the demon possessed, and raise the dead. He gave sight to the blind and hearing to those who had none. Being the only one without sin, he forgave others their sins. He came for the sinful, for he is the only One who is good, and came to save those who could never save themselves. Jesus came on a rescue mission, to make a living sacrifice at the cross, showing God's great love for sinners. After serving mankind, teaching, and performing many miracles, he went and suffered abuse after being unjustly accused by wicked men, and was nailed to a cross, and left to hang till death. He absorbed God's wrath for sinners that day, as he bore the weight of sin for sinners like us, and then breathed his last. Jesus did it to break sins curse, that believers would not face God's righteous judgment. He did it and then rose from the dead on the third day. The Lord did so to pay for my wickedness, and innumerable sins. His sacrifice, so long ago, reverberate down to this very day. Indeed, the Light of the World, Jesus, has shined upon us.

Holy God was pleased to reveal his Son to me, though I did not deserve it. Indeed, none deserve salvation, *'for all have sinned and fall short of the glory of God,'* (Romans 3:23) and *'...the wages of sin is death, but the free gift of God is eternal life in Christ Jesus our Lord.'* (Romans 6:23) He granted a wicked man like me, a new life. Jesus paid for all of my very many sins upon the cross, and God chose to bestow his benefits upon me by his unmerited favor, through faith. I confessed with my mouth that Jesus is Lord, and believed in my heart *'...that God raised him from the dead ... (Romans 10:9).* This gift from above, in 2010, is when everything changed. That was the day I was born a second time. Jesus said, *'..."Truly, truly, I say to you, unless one is born again he cannot see the kingdom of God."'* (John 3:3)

Thank God he has caused me to be born again. *'...Not because of works done by us in righteousness, but according to his own mercy, by the washing of regeneration and renewal of the Holy Spirit'* (Titus 3:5). Indeed, *'So then it depends not on human will or exertion, but on God, who has mercy.'* (Romans 9:16) He transformed all of my life. Under no self-compulsion of trying to clean myself up, but by the Holy Spirit freely given, God changed my heart, my mind, and my mouth. He changed my desires that were bent on hell and sin, and gave me a hunger and thirst for righteousness, and to honor him with my body. He provided the fruit of the Spirit, which is love, joy, peace, patience, kindness, goodness, faithfulness, gentleness, and self-control. Jesus gave me a hatred of sin in my life, and a love for that which is good in God's sight. I knew God was to be first in all things, and love him above all, and love all my fellow human beings, no matter what they believed, too. The things I would take in with my eyes, and reach for with my hands, and meditate on with my mind, and listen to are all different, for God made me new, transforming me, and granted me his awesome presence, through the Holy Spirit sent by Jesus Christ, who is here that I may walk in righteous steps, and there for me when I fall short, and loving me through it all. He is the One who is directing my life, for my good and his glory, and put me to his service, to proclaim this gospel, and to serve my brothers and sisters in Christ. He is the One who granted me eternal life. I have complete confidence that I will live with him forever, because of his very great promises, when my last appointed day comes to an end here, and I finish my course, the direction and purpose he has given for my life. So, I give God all the glory for it all, and for the many victories he has provided from my many sinful addictions.

I know that a birthday, as all days, are to give glory to God, for he is surely due. I love what our Lord Jesus said. ' ... *"The time is fulfilled, and the kingdom of God is at hand; repent and believe in the gospel."' (Mark 1:15)* Change your mind, and believe that Christ died for you, and rose from the dead. Believe in the only way of salvation and peace with God. Give him the glory, the only One who can save, for he is worthy of all honor and praise. Amen!

52

He is the One

Every broken heart, identity crisis, false thought, and suffering endured by a person that receives Christ, and believes on his name, are delivered from their hopelessness, to finding their hope—hope in him. The things we wanted ourselves to be known for are exchanged for having our identity found in the person of Jesus, the One who has '...*borne our griefs and carried our sorrows...' (Isaiah 53:4)*. He is the One who '...*is near to the broken hearted and saves the crushed in spirit.' (Psalm 34:18)* He is near to orphans, the fatherless, widows, and the poor, and also not far from any one of us. He is there for the hopeless at the end of their rope, and of these, lifts up those who are bowed down in humility.

He brings near those grieving due to afflictions of all kinds, and weighed down due to their sins. He calls to himself those who are known for their sinful reputations, and washes them clean from their dark past and guilt, filling them with his good and excellent Spirit. He brings low the religious and high minded, who sought to impress God and others by their own deeds and self-righteousness, humbling them by showing them their inability to save themselves, and granting them forgiveness through faith in Christ. He brings near people, no matter where they were in their thinking, and transforms them, making them children of God, completely unworthy of this awesome gift, but graciously granted by the gift giver, known as the Father of Lights. God's love is made known by the gospel, and the gift of faith granted freely to all who would, by his grace, believe.

He takes us away from the old life separated from God that went through the motions and sought temporal carnal desires, and brings forth the new and eternal, that is vibrant and from heaven itself; God coming to reside within our hearts by pouring in the gift of the Holy Spirit, who proceeds from the Father, and is sent by Jesus. The Holy Spirit that Jesus baptizes us with is the guarantee and seal of our inheritance with Christ, if we be God's children, bringing to mind the words of Christ, producing spiritual fruit in our lives, and providing spiritual gifts for service, while teaching and leading us in all truth.

He is the One who transforms life, delivering from the spiritual death, separation, and stupor we lived in prior to knowing the Lord, and brings forth revelation of who God is, and that we who know the Son are his. He is gracious to save people from every color and ethnicity, no matter prior religious affiliation, belief, or unbelief. Jesus is the One who said to a man who was drawn near to him, '...*"You are not far from the kingdom of God."*...' (Mark 12:34) The lost who are whole-heartedly searching, are the ones revealed drawn to, and found by the wonderful seeking Savior.

Jesus is the One who reveals the Father, the invisible God, being in perfect agreement with him, for '...*God is One...* (James 2:19). The Father sent his eternal Son, whom he loves, who the Father made everything through, and for, including the creating of each and every one of us. Christ teaches us how to pray to the Father, as he did, praying directly to him, and we learn in God's word that we do so, give thanks, and make our requests to our Father, through, and in the name of Jesus. Indeed, no one comes to the

Father except through the Son, for he is the One Mediator in heaven between God and mankind who will judge the living and the dead, for all authority in heaven and on earth was given him, because he purposefully came to suffer and die to purchase salvation for sinners. Jesus is the One with the name above all names, who was raised, and ascended back to the Father, and is seated at his right hand, who after the coming Day of Judgment will establish his heavenly kingdom upon the earth, which will be made new and imperishable, where only righteousness will dwell, sin eradicated, and suffering and death be no more.

Jesus is the Head of his blood bought, Spirit filled church, believers in Christ known as his body, whom he cares for, nourishes, watches over, and protects, shepherding over each member of the body faithfully as the Good Shepherd. He is the Rock in which we profess and believe, the firm foundation which his church is built upon.

He is the One who is the fulfillment of the word of God regarding the Messiah, the Anointed One who will come and save, promised by the Creator to the ancient patriarchs, Abraham and King David, through prophecy. He was promised not only to the people of the Jews who have believed, as King of the Jews, but also as King of Kings, being the hope for the peoples from every tribe, tongue, and nation of the earth, known as the Gentiles, *"For God so loved the world..."* *(John 3:16).* That Abrahamic and Davidic promise of God to the patriarchs of old, that through their ancestral line would come the Messiah, came to Joseph, their descendant generations later, by what happened to the woman named Mary, of whom Joseph was legally pledged to be married. An angel sent by God spoke to the virgin bride to be, and said to her, *'...**"Do not be afraid, Mary, for you have found favor with God. And behold, you will conceive in your womb and bear a son, and you shall call his name Jesus. He will be great*** *and will be called the Son of the Most High. And the Lord God will give to him the throne of his father David...' (Luke 1:30-32).* Mary conceived while still a virgin by the power of the Holy Spirit, sent from heaven to earth, that the Son of God would be brought forth. This awesome promise to the patriarchs was fulfilled by the legal covenant of marriage to Joseph prior to the birth of the Son of God, with their marriage consummated only after the Messiah's birth, waiting as a married couple on the promise of God in Jesus, who is also known by this prophetic and ancestral lineage, as the Root of David. This awesome hope for all the peoples is realized through that sign of this miracle birth, prophesied over 700 years B.C., through the prophet Isaiah, who said '...*the Lord himself will give you a sign. Behold, the virgin shall conceive and bear a son...' (Isaiah 7:14).*

It is this promised One, at about thirty years of age, who began his glorious ministry. He was attested by God with signs and wonders. Through these signs and wonders, such as making water turn into wine, performing miracles of healing, delivering people oppressed and possessed by demons, raising people from death, and feeding thousands miraculously, he revealed his omnipotent power over the natural with the supernatural, manifesting his glory.

He broke bread with the sinful, like prostitutes and tax collectors. These collectors of the tax were Jews, but were considered traitors by the Jewish people, for they collected money for the Roman occupiers, and taxed the people of Israel extra, to line their pockets and become rich. He came to where they were, and proclaimed the gospel of the kingdom of God, and taught them, showing his great love for people, for there are none righteous in and of themselves, and none without sin. The religious hypocrites of their day, known as the scribes, chief priests, Pharisees, and Sadducees, hated Jesus, for he was proclaiming the gospel, forgiving sins, teaching with authority, performing miracles, and many followed and believed in him. He also did not submit to their man-made teachings, limited understanding, or traditions, for they were not in line with the word of God. They looked at Jesus as a threat to their authority and their future. They were jealous, and sought to discredit, dissuade, and kill him. They were proud, and looked condemningly down on those who Christ ministered to, who they knew and shunned because of their prior sinful reputations, and were not in their high positions. Jesus rebuked them in many ways for their hypocritical, unrepentant, and disbelieving hearts. He said to, and of them, '..."Truly, I say to you, the tax collectors and the prostitutes go into the kingdom of God before you."' (Matthew 21:31)

The people were stunned with what he miraculously did. The blind he made to see, the deaf to hear, and the contagious lepers he touched and made clean. And as many as came to him, he healed them all, as they believed. He did it in fulfillment of his word which says, that '..."He took our illnesses and bore our diseases."' (Matthew 8:17) Most importantly, the people were astonished with what he taught, and with divine authority, as with the same power of the Holy Scriptures given by God in the Old Testament that bore witness about him. Crowds followed him wherever he went, to see him, touch him, and hear him.

He is the same Lord who graciously heals us plagued with the disease of sin, blind to our condition, and unable to hear what is good, and quickens us through the gospel, granting spiritual sight, and discerning ears, to awaken from spiritual death and unto new life eternal. 'Jesus Christ is the same yesterday and today and forever.' (Hebrews 13:8)

He is the One who is compassionate and merciful, '...slow to anger and abounding in steadfast love and faithfulness.' (Psalm 86:15) He is the Savior who wept, when one of his disciples wept before him, grieving over her brother who was dead four days, before Jesus raised him bodily, to life, from death. He also is the One who came upon that favored city of God, apart from any merit of the people, Jerusalem, and wept because of the unbelief of the majority of the people in their long awaited Messiah, refusing to lovingly come to him, by faith, which makes for peace with God.

He is the One who taught us the greatest of all commandments, which is, *"'...you shall love the Lord your God with all your heart and with all your soul and with all your mind and with all your strength.' The second is this: 'You shall love your neighbor as yourself.' There is no other commandment greater than these.'"* (Mark 12:30-31) If we have truly turned from our sins, to the Savior, by faith, we shall keep Christ's commandments, not by compulsion, but in loving devotion, for he said, *'..."If anyone loves me, he will keep my word, and my Father will love him, and we will come to him and make our home with him. Whoever does not love me does not keep my words. And the word that you hear is not mine but the Father's who sent me."* (John 14:23-24) Indeed, *'whoever says he abides in him ought to walk in the same way in which he walked.'* (1 John 2:6)

Our Lord teaches us to love fully, and from the heart, loving our enemies sacrificially, and to pray for our persecutors. He is kind to the just and the unjust, and his kindness is meant to lead us to repentance. He said, *'..."Love your enemies and pray for those who persecute you, so that you may be sons of your Father who is in heaven. For he makes his sun rise on the evil and on the good, and sends rain on the just and on the unjust. For if you love those who love you, what reward do you have? Do not even the tax collectors do the same? And if you greet only your brothers, what more are you doing than others? Do not even the Gentiles do the same? You therefore must be perfect, as your heavenly Father is perfect."'* (Matthew 5:44-48)

He taught us to forgive the trespasses of others all their trespasses, for we who believe have been forgiven all our sinful trespasses, for

Jesus paid for all of our sins. We who have been forgiven much, by Jesus, love much. Indeed, there is no question that as Christians we must forgive. God has entered our lives, and melted the hardest of hearts, inclining us to him, and pouring his love in.

He is the One known as the Bridegroom who came for his bride, his church of believers, who he has purchased for himself with the dowry of his own blood. He cleanses his people through that which he sacrificially shed on the cross, and washes them clean from guilt, for he bore the destructive stains of sin for them all, that we may be clothed in the gift and purity of his righteousness.

Jesus, the sinless Savior, who abhors sin, is also the gracious One who forgave a woman who the scribes and Pharisees brought before him, seeking Jesus to condemn her to being stoned to death for being caught in the act of adultery. We find when men condemn and forgive not, Christ forgives the repentant and believing. The One who told her, *"'...go, and from now on sin no more,'"* (John 8:11) is the One we approach in prayer, seated upon the throne of grace in the heavenly realm, who is our Advocate with the Father. We can come to him if we fall short, and remain with him throughout the day, by his love and meritless favor. We *are not* without, for he is the One called Immanuel, *'...(which means, God with us).'* (Matthew 1:23) He is with all who have turned from sin, and do not remain living in it, but by the righteousness that comes through faith. For all who continue in a lifestyle of sin have never known him, for all who believe have *'... died to sin...'* (Romans 6:2), and are *'...born of God.'* (1 John 3:9)

'...He had no form or majesty that we should look at him, and no beauty that we should desire him.' (Isaiah 53:2) He had no drastically distinct physical feature that set him apart from other men. He was not a foot taller, or the most handsome that we should follow him, for he had a body of flesh just like us. He looked like he could be a son of any other man, and of his many names, also called himself

Son of Man, because he came in the likeness of men, to make the sinless sacrifice that could deliver sinful sons of men. But Son of Man is not the only son he was, or else he could do nothing to deliver the soul. He is also known as the eternal Son of God, who is God, being perfectly One with the Father in glory, majesty, and Divinity, being Lord over salvation for sons of men.

He is the One who takes away confusion and distress, bringing peace, for he is the Prince of Peace. He breaks our chains that bound us to the things of this world, and delivers us from death, unto life everlasting. He is risen indeed! He illuminates the way, shining his spiritual light upon us, for he is the Light of the World. Even the fear of bodily death is no longer, for he has taken it away, for he is the Eternal Life who said, *"'The thief comes only to steal and kill and destroy. I came that they may have life and have it abundantly.'" (John 10:10)* He is also known as the Resurrection and the Life, and our boast is in him. He is greater than all of creation, and none is as high, for he is Lord of Lords. He is meek, and majestic, glorious and good. Who is like our God? He is unlike all others, for there are no gods, but One, and will not be removed from his throne. There are none other who can supernaturally turn one hair white or black other than he, knowing their full number, and on each ones' head. He, the promised One, is also the promise keeper, and all God's promises *'...find their Yes in him.' (2 Corinthians 1:20)*.

Christ breaks down our pride, and humbles his people like little children, as he said, *'..."Truly, I say to you, unless you turn and become like children, you will never enter the kingdom of heaven."' (Matthew 18:3)* He is with us, even when we are in trouble, and sees us through the trials of life. He gives us hope, and a future, for he himself is the Blessed Hope, and eternity is in his hands. He speaks pure unwavering words of truth, and life, for he is the Prophet, greater than all other prophets born of women that were sent before, for they came speaking of him, in complete agreement with the error-free prophetic writings in Scripture that revealed the Messiah, before he ever came from heaven to fulfill his mission on the earth, for he was there prior to creation, being eternal, and having no end.

The One who was physically touched and looked upon as he walked on the earth and among the people he created, is known as The Author of Life, who brings us the true meaning and understanding of life's purpose; that we were made to glorify God. The Lord Jesus is also known as the Lamb of God, who is the best friend any of us could ever have, because he laid down his perfect life as a sinless and spotless sacrifice for his friends. He is well known as the Door, providing access to Father God, through himself, being the Way, the Truth, and the Life.

The battle lines we drew, and banners raised, to somehow distinguish our prideful uniqueness and thinking apart from our Creator, are traded for looking to our great God and Savior, and being found exalting in the One who defeated death, sin, and Satan, the enemies of our souls. He removes the dull veil that blinded us in darkness, revealing our true condition, pointing us by his people and word, through the gospel, to the truth, that we may see beyond the natural sight into the purity and light of the spiritual, coming to know our invisible God who reveals himself through the message of Christ in the word of truth, the Holy Bible.

He opens the gates to heaven, being our Great High Priest. He is the God of love, and the One who's way is perfect. Life and death are in his hands, and provides his power perfectly in the midst of our weakness. He grants his people victory, by faith, as a gift, for he has graciously provided it with his cleansing blood. He is worthy of all worship, honor, and praise. We give glory to the Father through the Son, and the Son through the Father, *'giving thanks always and for everything to God the Father in the name of our Lord Jesus Christ' (Ephesians 5:20).*

He draws us closer and closer, and is our help in times of trouble, and our sustainer throughout the day. He is the whole of life, it's central focus, for he is second to none, and every knee shall bow and tongue confess him, *'...to the glory of God the Father.' (Philippians 2:11)* There are none else who raises himself from the dead, and will one day bodily raise all who have breathed their last on the earth as we know it, some to everlasting life, and others to everlasting punishment.

We see his true witnesses, followers of Christ who have lives transformed, having their fulfillment in him, for he is the One who makes all things new, and continues with his people through life's journey in steps he had graciously prepared, paths of righteousness, that we should purposefully walk in them, doing the things he would have us to do. We love Jesus above all, and follow him. He is the One who grants his perfect righteousness, that God may see us through his Son, and love us as he does our Lord, who said, *'"...The Lord our God, the Lord is one."' (Mark 12:29)*

Jesus is the One who promises that the world will not continue as it does, and that the hidden things, evils, and injustices of this world will be met by the Judge, who does so righteously, not as with what mere *eyes* can see, or *ears* can hear, but *with perfect judgment*. Indeed, Jesus is the One who saves us from the wrath to come, and will be with us, his people, forever. He is the King who will one day say to his people, *'..."Come, you who are blessed by my Father, inherit the kingdom prepared for you from the foundation of the world."' (Matthew 25:34)* May we rejoice in God, both now, and forever and ever, for favor, forgiveness, and freedom are found in him.

If you still do not know Jesus as your Savior, I pray you would continue to seek him, for there is no other salvation apart from the Messiah. But if today you have saving knowledge of this great God and Savior, finding yourself counted among God's people, his elect, go and be baptized '*...in the name of the Father and of the Son and of the Holy Spirit' (Matthew 28:19).* May we love one another, and all the more so, which reveals to us and to the world that we are the children of God. Let us walk in a manner worthy of his calling, in holiness, humility, honor, and loving obedience, making our calling and election sure. The One who was tempted in every way, yet endured all temptation and suffering without committing sin, understands the trials and struggles we go through, and is there for his people. He tells us to spiritually pick up daily that which others fear or are ashamed of, our cross of reproach and suffering for Christ's sake, and faithfully follow him. May we who have come to know him, or have known him and continue to delightfully walk with him, be attentive and purposeful as we strive after, and rejoice together, with one mind, and voice, for just as God is One, so too are we with each other, as fellow chosen sojourners, as we shine as lights for Christ in this fallen world these last days. Let us be faithful to know him better, separating from our lives the things that are worthless, and tell all our neighbors of what the Savior has done for our souls, making him known. Worship the Lord, and lift up his name and gospel as a trumpet! Let us pray always, and fervently, immerse ourselves in the treasure of the word of God daily, and gather around like minded believers, for we are made for community, and to serve one another in all love. Blessed be the name of the Lord Jesus forevermore, who is known in the final book of the Bible, Revelation, as the Amen. Amen

"Amazing grace! How sweet the sound
That saved a wretch like me!
I once was lost, but now am found,
Was blind but now I see."

Notes

These verses contain the whole, or part of the verse. For the whole of the verse, I encourage you, please refer to the Holy Bible, and read all of it. I am pleased to have shared with you from the English Standard Version, by way of biblegateway.com. "Scripture quotations are from the ESV® Bible (The Holy Bible, English Standard Version®), copyright © 2001 by Crossway, a publishing ministry of Good News Publishers. Used by permission. All rights reserved." https://www.crossway.org/support/esv-bible-permissions/

Short Quotations from other resources were made with use of the 'Fair Use' rule of copyright law.

1   John Newton. "Amazing Grace." 1779. http://library.timelesstruths.org/music/Amazing_Grace/
2   *Scarface.* Dir. Brian De Palma. Perf. Al Pacino. Universal Pictures, December 9, 1983. Youtube. Web. 2 December 2015. https://www.youtube.com/watch?v=RNSnMFgNq1Q
3   Winston Churchill, "Men Occasionally Stumble Over the Truth, But They Pick Themselves Up and Hurry Off" *Quote Investigator: Exploring the Origins of Quotations* http://quoteinvestigator.com/2012/05/26/stumble-over-truth/ (accessed December 2, 2015)
4   C.S. Lewis. *A Grief Observed.* (city unknown) Numitor Comun Publishing 2014. PDBooks.ca. Great Books in Canadian Public

Domain, http://pdbooks.ca/pdbooks/english/L/Lewis-C-S--A-Grief-Observed/hb7qag_files/text/part0001.html#filepos41332 (Ch. 2. Line 82-84)

5   Frank Sinatra. "My Way." Re-written by Paul Anka. Reprise, 1969. LP http://www.songfacts.com/detail.php?id=8040

6   Elvis Presley (date unknown) http://www.legacy.com/news/explore-history/article/elvis-quotes

7   Oprah Winfrey. Oprah Denies Jesus is the Only Way to Salvation & Heaven. Youtube. Web. uploaded February 11, 2011 https://www.youtube.com/watch?v=noO_dCWtB1E (accessed December 3, 2015)

Printed in the United States
by Baker & Taylor Publisher Services